ECHOES
CONTEMPLATIONS OF A MATURE RUNNER

BY:

MICHAEL BEISTY

Disclaimer

Content herein does not constitute specific advice to the reader's circumstance. It is only an opinion based on the author's and the publisher's perspective that others may learn from.

Anyone of any age who engages in running, and related exercise, should be in tune with their body and seek medical advice before embarking on an exercise program (including changes to said program) that may unduly extend them. This is critical should the aspiring athlete have underlying medical conditions and/or ongoing health issues requiring medication.

The author and the publisher is not a qualified medical practitioner or accredited coach. The information provided is not intended as medical advice or to replace advice given by trained medical or allied health professionals or qualified coaches. The author and the publisher give no warranty and make no representation that the information is suitable for any purpose or is free from error and accepts no responsibility for any person relying or acting on the information in this book, and disclaim all liability for any loss, damage, cost or expense incurred by reason of any person using or relying on the information or by reason of any error, omission, defect or misstatement contained in such information.

Acknowledgement of Country

This book was written in large part on the lands of the Awabakal people.

I acknowledge the history and Traditional Owners of the land on which I live and extend my respect to Elders past, present and emerging. I recognise their connection to Country and their strength and wisdom in caring for and maintaining Country over thousands of years.

Wherever I run and write, it always was and always will be Aboriginal Land.

Foreword

For a long time, I've been a strong advocate for strategies that encourage people of all ages to move more. Running, famous for its simplicity and purity, is top of the list when it comes to movement choices. It provides an enormous physical and mental health bang for your buck, is relatively cheap, accessible and easy to get started.

So, if running is really that good, how can we convince people of all ages to run more while ensuring it is both enjoyable and sustainable? The carefully curated collection of thoughts on running offered in this book is a great start to achieving this. Within these pages are sensible strategies which, if heeded, can enhance one's ability to run regularly and with enjoyment right up to, and throughout 'old age', however you choose to define it.

It was probably at the start or finish line of Newy parkrun that I met Mike, in the back half of 2012, the early stages of the event's life. Our paths crossed thanks to two key elements: a shared love of running and a shared habitat – the city of Newcastle, New South Wales, part of the Hunter Region, ambitiously dubbed the 'Region of Runners'.

I remember speaking with Mike in 2013 at an event I helped organise at the Newcastle Yacht Club. The event featured a panel of speakers including Olympic 5000m silver medallist Sonia O'Sullivan, Olympic marathoner Scott Westcott, a local running coach in his early 60s – Alan McCloskey – and Mike's father, Jim.

Jim was a long-serving coach and an accomplished, self-labelled 'sub-elite' runner in his own right, who at that stage was regularly completing local parkruns as a septuagenarian. Perhaps fittingly, given the theme of this book, the event was called 'running and longevity'. I remember Mike sitting at the back of the room, alongside other stalwarts of the Newcastle running community, engaged by the discussion and no doubt reflecting on his own and others' thoughts about the secrets of successfully combining running and ageing.

I've been fortunate to gain insight into Mike's thoughts over the past two decades via many articles he has penned for Run 4 Your Life magazine and Runner's Tribe. At times I felt Mike's words were specifically directed at me, providing timely advice and guidance, as I'm sure countless others have felt.

As in many parts of Australia, Newcastle is fortunate to lay claim to many senior runners training and competing at parkruns, at the track and at other organised events. Respectfully referring to this group as 'running elders', these enthusiasts help to normalise physical activity in the later years, proving that with careful planning, running and ageing can be successfully combined.

Clearly, Mike is an advocate for and a key member of this group of running elders. In his book, Echoes, Mike generously and helpfully shares the findings and results of extensive research and experiments he has conducted over his two running careers. Regardless of running age or stage, I believe the stories, advice and lessons within this book will ultimately lead to enormous benefit for the runner reading it.

A line I remember hearing during the panel discussion that night in 2013 has stuck with me since: 'We don't stop running because we get old. We get old because we stop running.'

Even though we may slow a little as more candles appear on the cake each year, I believe running ultimately keeps us young. Pursuit of the goal to continue running, or moving, for as long as our bodies allow us, is indeed a worthy one.

Enjoy the read and don't stop running!

Dave Robertson

Passionate runner, physiotherapist, running technique coach, teacher, athletics commentator, founder Newy parkrun

TABLE OF CONTENT

Introduction

I am 65 years old, still competing, and retired from employment.

I have written this book from the perspective of a mature person reflecting on a current and past enjoyment of running and racing. This collection is the culmination of a series of articles written and revised over several years, some previously published, some not. The final product points to a lived experience, contemplative of my running life and association with Australian distance running while residing in Newcastle, New South Wales.

My background consists of two distinct running careers. The first from the age of 12-30 (1970-1988) and the second recommencing in 2006, aged 47, and my writing reflects this dichotomy. In my first career I'd describe myself as a good-class club runner who failed to reach his potential. In my Masters career I have performed consistently at a national standard based on age grade calculations. My late father, Jim, was an avid distance runner and respected coach. My mother, Sue, was an early pioneer of Australian women's marathon running.

While this book is one of reflection, I have also introduced my concept of a Soft Quality Program (SQP) for mature distance runners. I anticipate publishing books about SQP under the banners of *Main Training Principles for Mature Runners* and *Mature Distance Runners: A Practical Philosophy*. They will provide greater detail of the program and how it works in practice for the competitive amongst us, an approach that is 'easy on the legs, easy on the mind'.

I would like to acknowledge the running community and the particular distance runners who have inspired my writing. The reader may notice that I sometimes refer to those who have passed, some of the characters and greats of our sport. I would usually prefix their names with the descriptor of 'late' but given that my writing is steeped in the past, and many names appear, that would become farcical. Respectfully, I have foregone the use of such a descriptor, preferring to think of them as though they are still with us, in their prime, and inspiring us now as they have always done.

I thank Mitchel Brown and Steve Landells, editors of the now defunct magazine *Run for Your Life*, and Ross Johnson, editor and cofounder of *Runner's Tribe*, for their respective leaps of faith in providing me, sight unseen, with platforms to write about running, the thing that I love.

I have written with optimism spliced by the reality of ageing and tempered by the non-running objectivity of my wife, Mandy. I trust you will enjoy the reading as much as I have enjoyed the writing.

Michael Beisty

Soft Quality Dissected: A Masters Dimension

During my sixth decade on this earth, I was engaged in a rebirth of sorts, returning to distance running on a competitive level, albeit low key. And during this time, I explored running carrying the baggage of my youth, but with eyes open and prepared to learn how to get the best out of myself as a mature person. This meant 10 years of introspection and research, expanding my knowledge through reading and experimentation in my training. A lived experience if you like, to develop a program targeted to the fifties that can be adjusted to the forties, and adapted to the sixties and beyond.

My basic premise is, and continues to be, questioning what we are told by the experts through this lived experience. Everyone is different, but also the same. There can be no denying that macro concepts apply to ageing and running but there is always room at the edges to determine what best fits your personal circumstance. The development of a 'better fit' training program for Masters entailed critical thinking about what I was doing and why. To help me along the way I drew upon the practical philosophers of mainstream training systems like Arthur Lydiard, Percy Cerutty and Tim Noakes and the Masters knowledge base of such eminent practitioners as Peter Reaburn, Joe Friel, Earl Fee, and Cathy Utzschneider.

And I think I have done it well, within reason. But it's not about a set schedule. It's about a broad framework of principles, or a nuanced approach, that a mature distance runner can plan within and test how mainstream concepts of ageing and running may or may not apply to their particular situation. This training system is not meant to provide all the answers but assists in identifying touchpoints that could warrant further investigation by the reader. It provides an opportunity to learn about yourself, the person who really matters, and what actually works for you.

The final product is what I call a Soft Quality Program (SQP), targeted to mature distance runners in their fifties competing at five kilometres to half marathon. In many ways it is similar to the

Australian complex training system promulgated by Pat Clohessy and others, premised on Lydiard principles, and tailored to the mature competitor.

Essentially, a SQP focuses on endurance as an ideal way of building aerobic capacity while at the same time enabling a degree of performance progression. Put simply, my concept of a SQP is to include faster than steady pace running, primarily no faster than five kilometres race pace, on a regular but less structured basis, all year round. A SQP relies on feel and effort as opposed to time and distance, and is more easily adapted to natural surroundings. You search for grasslands and ovals, dirt trails and parklands that allow fast and controlled running and steer away from the track. You only train once per day and maintain reasonable but not excessive weekly mileage: for example, 40-50kmpw for the beginner and 80-90kmpw for the experienced and 100-120kmpw for the elite.

A SQP is mildly stretching, supports progression in performance year on year but doesn't exhaust the mature athlete, physically or mentally. The regularity of this sort of lower quality (but above steady state) running is more challenging than it may seem. Yet it is also an ideal way to ensure some intensity in your training without it feeling onerous.

The Essential Elements of SQP

- Use of fortnightly to four-weekly training cycles.

- A taper week: every fifth week halve your mileage to consolidate the previous block of training and have a rest day this week if you feel the need.

- Train in natural surroundings and on grass or dirt as much as possible – for steady continuous runs and faster work.

- Rely on perceived effort and run as much as possible without timing your reps.

- Integrate strength work into the program, as additional training, not as a replacement to running. Incorporate stretch band and whole of body strength exercises every second or third day to ensure mobility, flexibility and strength, and as an injury prevention strategy.

- Conduct regular hill running to build leg strength and ankle flexibility.

- Err towards a smaller number of repetitions for anything above 600, at slightly faster than 5km race pace/effort eg 3x800, 3x1km, 2x1600, 2x2km.

- Conduct shorter repetitions (200-600) at 5km race pace/effort with a higher number of reps and short rest intervals eg 8-10x400, 200 jog.

- Use 'real' fartlek. This can be your toughest session. Challenge yourself to include hard surge efforts at different speeds or over undulating courses, say the middle 6km of a 12km run.

- Intermittent use of pure speedwork running short reps at close to maximum effort, with long rest breaks, to develop sprinting capability. These sessions are gradually introduced as part of a phased approach within SQP, typically during a heavy racing or freshening up period. This high-end fast work will help fire up type II fast twitch muscle fibres beneficial for shorter racing. They will also assist by improving cadence for race performance over 5km to 10km distances. Careful management is required to negate risk of injury.

- Use anaerobic lactic training sparingly as part of a transitional phase to a 'freshening up' peak racing period.

- Judicious use of tempo runs at 5-10km.

- Over time, let your steady runs build to faster paces if the urge arises but don't be afraid to have gentle runs to ensure adequate recovery.

- To enable reasonable pace, long runs are limited to 16km, increasing to 20km twice per week (Wed/Sun) if training for half marathons.

- Run the second half of your Sunday long run significantly faster than the first and kick down the last 2km.

- Have three days steady running between particularly hard efforts/sessions.

- Race at distances of 5km or less at least every fortnight at your local club or Masters event, or parkrun; and

- Use race performance to gauge progression.

When using a SQP you can expect the speed of your training to increase for the same effort expended as you progressively work through the blocks of training. Your mileage may increase incrementally in tandem with your speed capability, though significant increases in mileage are not essential. You may find big improvements in race outcomes if you choose to have a hard race at the end of your taper week.

A Sixties Approach

I am now 65 years of age and unfortunately, I have suffered some injuries in my early sixties that has dinted my progression, caused by ageing factors rather than the act of running itself. However, this has provided me with valuable lessons about how to tailor my SQP for this decade of running and racing, a sixties approach.

As I write this article, I continue to refine the SQP. Advice from sports scientist Peter Reaburn is a game changer for mature distance runners. He suggests that mature competitors who have engaged in a lifetime of 'chronic' high intensity training and racing forego 'at threshold and above' continuous running in favour of interval training. Based on contemporary research, Reaburn considers this to be an optimal approach for speed development to reduce the risk of adverse cardiac health outcomes. He is concerned that a mature runner not flog themselves for long periods of time, instead adopting a program of mild to moderate distance training of lesser volume with hits of higher intensity interval training sessions, say 10 x 400, once per week.[1]

Reaburn considers that mature runners, particularly from their fifties onwards, should transition to a philosophy of valuing exercise as medicine, with a lesser frequency of high intensity training and racing.

Using the fifties SQP as a base template, with Reaburn's insights in mind and remembering this is geared towards an elite competitive distance runner, my tailoring for the over sixties includes:

- Run the easy runs easier.

- Include more active recovery days. My personal preference is for slower and shorter easy runs, rather than cross training or rest days, to maintain consistency in running and the routine of a daily run.

- Lift 'heavy' weights to build strength in upper and lower body up to three times per week and include deadlifts for all round strength.

- Dispense with continuous threshold and tempo runs and focus moreso on interval training.

- Dispense with anaerobic lactate training.

- Use short hill repetitions to replace speed sessions and hilly courses for steady state aerobic runs to enhance durability.

- One core session of faster work per week, and contingent upon race commitments definitely no more than two. Alternate between fartlek, short hill reps and interval sessions.

- Use of what I call rhythm sessions for longer repetitions of 800 metres and above at 5km race pace, or typically at half to three quarters perceived effort, with short rest intervals.

- Continue to use pure speedwork as described for the fifties' cohort.

- Scale back the overall frequency of racing and compete in distances of 10km or more only up to four times per year.

Longer injury healing time is a significant consideration that is often overlooked. For example, it can take double the time for a 60-year-old mature runner to heal and rehabilitate from a pulled hamstring, when compared to a 20-year-old, something that I have recently experienced. For a 75-year-old it may take three times longer.[2] As an aside, Reaburn states while repair to muscle, ligament, tendon and cartilage appears delayed with ageing, there is no evidence to indicate delays in bone repair following fractures.[3] The mantra is best not to get injured, and the refinements I have made into my sixties are an attempt to follow this mantra while maximising the enjoyment of running and racing into the future.

Welcome to My Nightmare Aka the Plight of the Mature Runner

'Argh!' I croaked, gasping more in desperation than effort as the bar came crashing down on my stomach. I must have held the bar above my chest for at least 20 seconds, willing the weight upwards, drawing on all my strength, but to no avail. I was pinned to the bench, my abdomen beginning to bruise.

I looked a sight lying in the backyard, my Labrador circling and nudging me in the face as I slid the barbell to the left of my body. Slowly, muscles cramping, I pushed the barbell diagonally upright. Holding it carefully, with all the remaining strength I could muster, I removed the free weights at one end and placed them on the ground. What blessed relief. No spotter, no brains. It could have gone terribly wrong.

My pitiful attempt to lift weights to forestall an inevitable loss of muscle and bone is one example of how mature athletes try to fight the ageing process. You see, our bodies fracture easily. We are either heading towards or recovering from injury and ailments, with only a small window of time in-between when we might be able to perform well. We don't have the luxury of always choosing periodisation. We are glad to run when we can, if we can.

You will notice many of us lilting, tilting, stooping, hunching, even falling, as we train and race to the best of our ability. Like wind-up toys we attempt fast repetitions, our pitter-patter cadence compensating for a shorter stride.

I often think how comical I must look as I pump out 400s at the local park. But what can I do? For me and my fellow Masters time is of the essence, so we must keep going.

We fool ourselves into believing we have a good core when it's clear for all to see that we have a good core of fat. The flab moves inexorably towards our middle, hanging there as a heavy reminder of our mortality.

We are stretching aficianados for no other reason than if we don't stretch, we can't run. Our Achilles tendons are brittle pieces

17

of rope, ready to snap when we rise in the morning. We excel at running the grass verges pulling ourselves along the suburban roads, ooh-ing and ah-ing the first few kilometres until the numbness drowns our pain. Then we can run. Oh, how we can run, six minutes kilometre pace if we are lucky.

We are always tired because we sleep less and are determined to maintain the mileage of our youth, taking at least 25 percent longer to do it. And while we run our reps hard, eyes bulging, we can never quite reach the anaerobic nirvana of those golden years.

When racing, our breathing isn't laboured because we can't dig deep enough. We breathe shallow rasps, in and out with the rapidity of a Gatling gun, as our pulmonary and cardiac systems adjust and readjust to the shocking intensity of running fast.

But we are also cunning. We are savvy trainers, making best use of our precious injury-free time with focused effort. In our races we want to beat the one percent of young 'uns who go off like scalded cats before falling in a heap 800 metres on. We wear shabby and tacky, yet comfortable gear, to throw our competitors off the scent. For us, there is no bigger buzz than beating the younger set in their designer gear, who mistake our grey hair and balding scalps for signs of decrepitude.

Perhaps most important of all, we are strong-willed and determined. Despite the growing reality of our nightmare, we continue to dream that we can achieve as we have before.

The Just Forties

Having returned to distance running in my late 40s, I missed the much-vaunted downturn in performance that coincides with turning 40. However, after much hypothesising, I am not convinced that this is as it should be. More and more I think this is a self-fulfilling prophecy to which many of us resign ourselves. But should we?

I have never quite understood why the over 30s are included in Masters classifications. I can already see some of you rolling your eyes because I'm sure previous generations of Masters athletes and the Masters movement itself has considered this issue ad infinitum – but maybe it's worth another look.

If you examine the performances of many in their mid to late 30s, you'd have to question the veracity of including an over 30 or over 35 Masters category for women or men (once upon a time described as pre-Vets).

When he addressed this issue in the 1970s, the American David Pain pulled no punches. An early promoter of the worldwide Veterans movement as it was known in 1971, Pain said, 'If the 30-39 group wants a program badly enough they should form their own organisation and do their own thing.' He asked insightfully, 'Do we want to make the younger men older, or the older men younger?'[4]

Despite such early protestations, the over 30s have become an accepted bottom-end age category of the Masters movement. It was a decision made in the name of inclusivity, I gather. But is it the best option for the advancement of absolute performance standards for the over 30s who are progressing into the Just Forties (J40s) performance zone?

I have always been perplexed about how some J40s play down their capacity to perform to a very high level in absolute terms. The inclusion of a Masters category for the '30s' may contribute to such an outlook. Accepting that we are old at 30 may be setting our sights too low, too early in our ageing process. I would argue that in our modern society the 50s are the new 40s. If Kenenisa

Bekele (Ethiopia) can run a marathon in 2:04:15 at age 41, and our own Sinead Diver can run 2:21:34, aged 45, why can't you?

A perverse aspiration is now prevalent, of aiming for strong performances in the first year of the next five-year age category three or four years out. This is tacitly endorsed by the adoption of five-year competitive categories. While it may be laudable that such ambition drives many to compete harder as they age, it also causes a subconscious resignation to lesser performances in the intervening years, 'keeping your powder dry' so to speak. This may not be of major concern for us real oldies, but I wouldn't want to encourage such an outlook for those in their 30s, approaching 40.

Having said all this, I must point out that Sir Roger Bannister emphasised the importance of mental strength in achieving high performance standards. He believed that the brain is the limiting factor in human exhaustion and the major determinant of how hard exercise systems can be pushed. He cited Tim Noakes as a co-proponent of his view.[5]

Sir Roger would have known, having been a successful international athlete who trained at high intensities, and a world-renowned neurologist, no less. Admittedly, he wasn't talking specifically about the performance of mature athletes, but the tenet that mental strength is the key attribute that makes or breaks absolute success in performance is difficult to argue, no matter what your age.

Isn't it possible for mental strength developed through years of distance training and competition to more than offset the loss of physical capacity caused by ageing?

While this is less credible for someone like me in my mid-60s, where the physical unquestionably overrides the psychological, it is not untenable for runners aged 35-42 to achieve more than they did at a younger age because they know themselves better, have developed more capacity to draw on their psychological strength and still have the physical capacity resembling their youth.

Although not totally logical – and who said we have to be logical? After all we are human – I prefer to keep looking backwards to what I have achieved, as an incentive to my performance today. I encourage the J40s to do the same, to keep that ambition for their best career performance flickering, just long enough to get the absolute best out of themselves. This opportunity will end soon enough without willing it to end.

Athletics history is sprinkled with many distance runners in their just or nearly 40s performing at a very high level in international championships or in absolute terms. Surely the advancement of distance running performance in the 35-44 years age bracket is the next major frontier of athletic endeavour, supported by advancements in psychological strategy?

It has already started, and mark my words, you ain't seen nothing yet.

Old Timer

I was out for my usual jaunt the other day, an easy one ambling along the Fernleigh track when I came upon a young guy running by. As runners often do, we ran together for a few kilometres and we got talking.

It was nice to converse with a member of the younger set, though he is now on the wrong side of 35. It's all relative. He said to me, 'It's great to see blokes like you still out training and racing. It's an inspiration to guys like me.' And he called me an 'old timer'. I know he meant it as a sign of respect and I took it that way, but I've thought on it long and hard. Old timer? What does that mean?

It could mean I'm gone and forgotten, or gone and just hanging on or gone, just gone and am nowhere to be seen, invisible to the world of competitive distance running.

Or it could mean that I'm a beacon, a signpost, a shining star, an example of what could be if you have the desire, commitment and motivation to get off your backside.

Old timer is anachronistic, a term no longer in vogue. We are not even Veterans. We are Masters or Seniors. That's more politically correct. But to the public we are used up, discarded, less relevant, can't work, won't work, don't work.

Old timer was meant as a compliment, but it felt like a putdown.

I was listening to a well-known Australian business woman on the radio recently. A woman of senior years herself, she had an interesting take on ageism. While 'mature' could have connotations of wisdom, knowledge and savvy, she hates the word, saying such a tag evokes images of 'a good wine, red and bloated', instead of emphasising the value of a 'lived experience'. OK, OK, I get it, but there could be worse descriptions of a red wine gone off.

And what about women? I mean, call me sexist, but old timer just doesn't fit. 'Old girl' is disrespectful, though that's what I used to call my mother. 'Old cheese' or 'old ched', a term of endearment as it became known in the Aussie vernacular of my younger years in the 1970s might be an apt descriptor. After all what better to go with red wine than cheese?

But I need to stop there because I know I'll get myself into trouble if I continue down this rabbit hole. Suffice to say I can't think of a comparable description for women distance runners of mature vintage. Maybe the reader can?

So, don't let the societal descriptors that devalue your lived experience affect your outlook on life and running. Don't let anyone tell you 'you can't do it', because then you won't do it. Don't believe them, believe your heart. Use your wisdom, use your age, let your 'red wine' breathe life into your life, and the life of others, and take you to where you want to be.

Built to Last

We've come a long way since Francie Larrieu's comments of 1974, spoken at the tender age of 21: 'Social pressure – that's the hardest thing we women in track have to overcome. People who see me training are always asking, "Aren't you a little old to be doing this kind of stuff?" It's very distressing. You would think I was still playing with dolls or something.'[6]

Francie was a prominent American distance runner and a four-time Olympian (1972-1992). Sadly, such remarks typified the attitude of many Western societies towards competitive women middle distance runners at that time.

However, the fun-running boom of the mid-1970s into the 1980s, and the explosion of recreational running in Australia and across the globe has created a more welcoming environment for women. This includes mature women attempting running for the first time.

Various research in the US has revealed an increasing trend for women of all ages to take up recreational running, mainly road running, with much lesser focus on competition (track or road). The number of women in road races has outstripped the participation rate of men. Certainly, I have noticed a very high proportion of women in parkruns and Australian running festivals. This makes sense, as it is a grassroots avenue for women to introduce themselves to the concept of exercise, and low-level running with an emphasis on community participation, and general health and wellbeing.

To the casual observer, the introduction of women's distance events at the Olympic Games appears hit and miss, with the marathon first run in 1984, four years earlier than the 10,000 metres (1988) and 12 years before the 5000 metres (1996). The USA and global road running boom saw women of all ages competing in races up to the marathon, and this may have countered conservative views about a woman's ability to run and race distance events, providing some momentum for the introduction of the longer distances first in the Olympic Games?

Undoubtedly, it was also the result of the lobbying powers of such luminaries as Kathrine Switzer and Dr Joan Ullyot.

Women's Olympic 800m final Amsterdam 1928. Lina Radke (Germany) beats Kinue Hitomi (Japan). Credit: Central Press.

However, it seems unfair that the marathon got the inside running into the Olympic arena, while track specialists were left languishing for many years. I can't help thinking that exaggerated reporting of the 1928 Amsterdam Olympic Women's 800m finalists' state of exhaustion had a lot to do with it. Such images may have echoed shrilly 50 years on in the minds of the fat controllers of the Olympic movement. Or it may simply be that introducing a new event requires agreement across all continents, and that's not easy. Or a combination of both? Who knows? But it is surely an inconsistency in running history that can't be objectively reconciled.

Now, I know there are some significant physiological differences between men and women. While I don't feel particularly qualified to talk about them, I have noticed that women in general, and this extends to the mature woman (compared to the older man), seem to perform particularly well at longer distances and ultra-events. It also appears that women's marathon performances tend to outstrip their performances at 10 kilometres. A cursory examination of most race results tells me so. And I've often wondered why.

Well, what the experts say about this has been pretty consistent over the past 40 years. Leaving the most obvious women's health issues alone, the most significant physiological factors that affect women's performance, compared to men, is the lower ratio of strength to weight (women having higher levels of fatty tissue and less muscle), a smaller heart, lower oxygen uptake and lesser oxygen-carrying capacity (lower haemoglobin concentration in blood).[7]

On a positive note, Ernst van Aaken, who pioneered Long Slow Distance (LSD), identified that more of women's total body weight is stored fuel and less is dead weight (muscle), with a beneficial effect on endurance.[8] Women have a small heart but in a light frame. Given their smaller size relative to men, this lends itself to better comparative performances in ultra-distance running. Women are physically incapable of burning glycogen as quickly as men because they lack the necessary muscle power.

Some authors surmise that women may be more efficient in metabolising body fat, before having to draw on glycogen stores, enabling greater levels of performance in endurance events such as marathons. This has been coined The Female Endurance Advantage.[9] Any such 'advantage' is impressive, given women have 10 percent less aerobic capacity than men and extra body fat that hinders endurance performance.[10]

Ultra-marathoner and naturalist Bern Heinrich has a different take on the proposition that women are better performed ultra-marathoners than men because women have more body fat. He makes the point that on average women are much slower than men and that for them to run as far and as fast as men, it requires a massive loss of body fat that inevitably results in the cessation of ovulation. In other words, there is a trade-off between performance and the ability to reproduce sexually, a perverse consequence of a love of running that men do not have to consider.[11]

In any event, it is self-evident that women can run closer to their maximum aerobic pace for longer than men and may do better, relative to their own capacities, where endurance rather than power (muscle) is important. In fact, it appears that women are built for distance running.[12]

However, while Masters runners of both sexes are advised to ensure adequate recovery from tough sessions by over-compensating for age, men do have a distinct advantage because of their higher levels of testosterone that assists muscle repair and growth. So, it's not unusual for senior women runners to require more easy days and longer recovery than their male counterparts of the same age.[13]

At age 40, there is a 15 percent performance gap between men and women. By age 60, this gap is 10 percent. While the slowdown for both genders during this period is linear, men's performance decreases more sharply thereafter, and women continue on a roughly linear downturn. Over this period, a trained woman should be able to edge out an untrained man.[11]

So, if you are a mature aged man lining up in your local parkrun or community running event, you should spare a thought for the women around you. If they are young and competitive, they will probably beat you, and if they are a bit older, they are sure to get you eventually, one way or another. It's just a matter of time.

In Search of the Real Sensation

Distance running delivers many sensations, some unexpected and others that should be anticipated, yet for some reason aren't. Age, level of fitness and mindset can colour our sensations.

On January 8, 1972, I competed in an Under 14 1500m interclub race at Olympic Park. Just turned 13, I had my first win for the Hunters and achieved my first sub-5.

There was something very peculiar about my experience. I'm sure it wasn't a runner's high, but it certainly was a weird sensation. As I rounded the final bend, I found myself floating along with no effort at all, not straining in that grounded, gritting your teeth fashion of a final sprint, but floating above my body watching myself run. I was an onlooker and competitor all in one.

It was an out-of-body experience (OBE). An OBE, known as an autoscopy, is not uncommon within the general populace.[15] I recollect talking to my father about it on our drive home. In his typical understated way, he said, 'That's all right, son, that's the beauty of running. You never quite know what's around the corner.' And he laughed, muttering that he could do with a change of body himself, but leave the mind alone. We never talked about it again, but it's something I've always been searching for, to repeat that weird but real sensation.

Mature runners arrive, or return, in their 40s, 50s, 60s and beyond, many from sedentary backgrounds, and often looking for a new sensation. Typically, some are making comebacks from a previous running career, crossing over to distance running as a new sport, or starting fresh as a distance runner without any lengthy sporting background. A few will be returning to running from past or recent injury. Some are searching for joy, others for health and to lose weight, and others for a means to satisfy their competitive drives.

My middle-aged running experience is like many. Running fell by the wayside in my 30s, but the lure was never too far away. Even as my weight ballooned into the high 90 kilograms, I had pride in my ability to step out the door at any stage and run 5km straight up. This was my test of basic fitness that allowed me to delude myself that I was still a runner and not a jogger.

Jack Foster (no. 1) leads Tom Fleming (no. 3) at the 1974 American Athletic Union Marathon Championships. Foster, aged 43, wins in 2:18:24. Credit: Lydiard Training and Academy website.

Fast forward to 2007, one year into my comeback at 48 years old, running four days a week, I decided to become more serious in my training. Part of my plans were to run regular 5km time trials at Nesbitt Park, a local grass track. For some reason, I thought I'd just be able to hit out at five-minute mile pace like I used to. Imagine my shock when my first mile split was 7:08. I eventually turned in a 23:35. I was gutted. It was a wake-up call from father time, and a reminder that hard graft is required if you are serious about achieving your potential. Gradually, though begrudgingly, I have come to accept the secret for mature runners is to live for the moment and not for the past. You can adjust your expectations without undermining the enjoyment.

For the mature person transitioning to running from other disciplines experienced when young, the adaptation required can be challenging. Running is running, and nothing can match its relentless demands on body and mind, especially in that early start-up phase. Distance and time go together and can be hard to fathom for the newcomer. 'I can't run fast enough, I can't run far enough, I can't run fast and far.'

Olympian Jack Foster in his booklet *Tale of the Ancient Marathoner*[16] relayed his early experience in an entertaining fashion. Jack was a club cyclist in England who immigrated to New Zealand and at 32 years of age thought he'd take up distance running.

In his first attempt, Jack intended to run for 30 minutes while on a family picnic. On his return from his run his wife asked, 'What's wrong, have you forgotten something?' To Jack's disbelief, he had been gone only seven minutes, even though he was sure he had run six or seven miles.

The ability to return from injury becomes harder as you age, but you will get back with persistence. Having been out of action for more than a year (but now on the way back) I know that the longer the break from running the more you are like a sedentary person, and you may need to treat your comeback that way.

Act conservatively, build sustainability. Build the base to enable necessary physical adaptation to provide some future protection against injury. And if you want to maximise your running performance, run every day, if possible, because consistency is the key. But also recognise that as you get older, decade to decade, you may need to over-cater for rest and recovery.

Given the level of adaptation required in middle age, does it feel different inside? How does your sensation of running differ in your 40s, 50s, and 60s? Or does it? There is much ado about the physical, physiological and biological changes that affect performance with ageing, but I haven't seen much written about how it feels inside, the bodily sensation. For me, although two minutes a mile slower, the sensations I feel when training are the same as when young. However, the physiological ceiling of age (lower maximal heart rate) becomes more apparent when racing.

During a race, I have noticed that settling into a rhythm takes longer than I'd like, my breathing can be more erratic during the initial stages, and my ability to crank it up to faster speeds can take a while. This gives a sensation of running short of oxygen more quickly.

When you are young, the racing sensation is about being able to draw immediately on raw unbridled power. When you are older, the racing sensation is more about searching for additional horsepower from an engine running on just two aerobic cylinders instead of four. Maybe this is why I've never again been able to repeat the OBE of my youth?

Or maybe I just achieved my perfect race where mind meets body at the tender age of 13?

Nowhere to Hide

I have always liked the feeling of running hard and fast. Unfortunately, as I've got older, how I feel and how it translates in terms of race performance are two very different things. I am a hopeless case. I need competition as an end game to provide focus for my training. I'm running slower, but my competitive desire remains strong. And there is nothing like track racing to heighten your competitive sensibilities.

Track racing is special. Track is hurt, in its purest form for all to see, where tactical prowess comes to the fore. You can test yourself in an absolute sense in an uncompromising arena where distance is accurate and the laps just keep on coming. It is where you achieve your real PBs and you can't fudge your times. In short, there is nowhere to hide. This is frightening stuff for some.

The thing about track racing is that everything is accentuated: your feelings about what you are about to do, and your expectations about what you should be able to achieve, whether to win or run a fast time. For some reason, pre-race nerves are tauter than for other racing disciplines, lactic appears on the scene quicker, and there is a sharper awareness of your opponent's movements. More often than not, the track arena causes you to channel your effort harder than you would on road, cross country, or trail. If your legs are still up to it, add in the wearing of spikes and you have no excuses for a poor performance.

Stickability is the quintessential challenge of track competition, whether attempting to maintain a pace from out front, trying to bridge a gap or hanging on to your nearest competitor. And you will have to fight hard to resist your subconscious tendency to slow in the home straight as you circle each lap. Track is where you see fear, desperation and control all rolled into one, a melodrama fit for television inevitably acted out in the last lap grunt as you and your rivals sail for home.

I know that for many, track racing is a turn-off. Who wants to race around in circles when there are plenty of other options for running? Isn't it boring? Isn't it embarrassing when you get lapped? Isn't it for younger people? Questions like these are typical of those who do not truly understand the allure of track racing.

And why so, you may ask.

Well, track requires a tough mental attitude towards competition, and an ability to continually monitor and be in tune with your body's reactions during the stress of racing. This is often described as strong association between mind and body.

However, many runners, particularly recreational and mature runners, practise high levels of dissociation, blocking out bodily feelings instead of focusing on them.[17] And there is nothing wrong with that. As Amby Burfoot points out, many older runners use their running pastime to get away from other life pressures. The last thing they want is another 'hurry-up race'.[18]

But for those of you who want to compete hard and fast, track competition is your ultimate test. This is where you find the war horses of the past, ex-internationals, 'good uns', reliving their glory days, and competing against the likes of you, in a local club event.

So, while I accept that there are plenty of other events you can race apart from track – and I know they all require mettle, perseverance and challenging training regimes to achieve success – they cannot replace the fierce, almost gladiatorial, contest that we call track racing.

No matter what your age, the competitive desire to win can burn white hot.

Speed to Burn

I often ponder the whys and wherefores of speed. I know I have never maximised my potential to run fast because I've never really had a go at improving my pure speed.

I think many of us neglect this area. It's not a nice fit for a distance runner's natural inclination, free-range running. There is never a right time to do pure speedwork right, unless you build it into a sharpening phase and create space for it in your competitive racing program.

While we all have an innate ability to run fast, and some of us need more help than others, I accept the mantra of 'use it or lose it' for the mature runner. Physiologically speaking, we need to remind our body constantly of what fast running feels like because as we age, the body more easily forgets. Certainly, the ability to dig out a really fast last 400 off a high-base training regime has become more difficult as I have aged.

During my first running career from age 12 to 30, I experimented unsuccessfully with mixes of speed and distance training. For instance, I ran 4:02 for 1500 a few days after turning 18 yet my best ever was only 3:58. This experimentation ranged from low mileage/high anaerobic, to high mileage/low anaerobic, to periodisation, to what was colloquially described in Australia during the 1970s and '80s as complex training (where you did all types of training during a one-week or two-week continuous cycle). However, there was always one ingredient missing: pure speedwork.

Since then, I have come to believe that pure speedwork sessions in addition to necessary anaerobic work is the magic ingredient to achieving your potential in distance running – but always based on the assumption you have achieved the necessary aerobic base.

That's not a particularly enlightened statement, I can hear you say, but I'm constantly amazed how so many athletes commit to high-intensity training programs without recognising the need for an adequate base, particularly those who specialise in middle distances.

In my second running career I have searched for a happy medium between quality work and distance, recognising that being older I'm more prone to injury. In local Masters circles, I hear many talking about running less mileage and having more rest, but running faster in their daily sessions. I also know there are some elite Masters distance runners, men and women, doing some mind-boggling quality sessions with good results and without excessive mileage.

The one thing I have appreciated more with age is that the ability to strike the right balance between pure speed and distance is an art, not a science. It is intuitive, relying on the runner understanding his/her body and the way it responds to stimulus. We all know what our own natural tendencies are on the spectrum of pure speed and endurance. For instance, I tend towards endurance and longer distance. We need to work this equation to our benefit in devising our training programs, but never moving too far away from quality.

For the mature runner, uninhibited speed play by use of fartlek, doing untimed interval sessions in natural surroundings, and having more regard to perceived effort, provides an opportunity to run hard and fast on a less-structured basis.

Combined with judicious use of tempo runs of 5km and 10km, I've found this a useful approach to building quality sessions back into my program after injury, bringing me back to pre-injury performance levels quite quickly. Such training can provide a solid platform for mature runners, and some preliminary hard wiring, to the pure speedwork that should come later. Psychologically, it is less taxing, yet physically it can be quite demanding.

To run really fast, it is not good enough just to do anaerobic work. You need to do speedwork where you run very fast over distances as short as 30m and no longer than 150m, with long rest intervals. You can't run fast if you're doing high mileage. Don't even try it. You need to do this work in low-mileage periods, typically when sharpening or peaking, or 'coming on' as they used to say in days gone by.

To get the best out of yourself, it is essential to leave pure speedwork to periods when you are racing fresh, and peaking for a particular race, or series of races. As a 50s-plus distance runner, I experienced first-hand the benefits of pure speedwork and working on technique. Over two months, at 55 years old, I used pure speedwork to great effect, gradually reducing my weekly 5km parkrun times from 17:40s to 17:13, simply by including one session per week like 10 x 100, 10 x 50/50 accelerations, 6 x 120 to 150, all with long rest intervals. My weekly volume was never much more than 80km per week.

Rest assured, as you teach your body to run fast, this requires perseverance and a positive mind-set. You can expect a level of discomfort in your buttocks, hamstrings, groin and stomach as your body adapts to running fast. If you are a 'slow twitcher' like me, during early sessions you will feel clunky.

Initially, you'll find that your legs can't keep up with your arms. But if you concentrate on form or technique, and running relaxed at pace, letting your legs be pulled through by your arms, you will gradually transcend to another level of efficiency at speed. Suddenly it will click, and your 5km and above race pace feels slow.

All you need to do is give it a go and you will have speed to burn.

Not Negotiable

How often do you think about not running? A peculiar question to ask you might say. But once you reach a certain age this consideration starts to raise its head. Not being able to run ever again is not something we want to contemplate. It's confronting, but as we age, the reality of maintaining our physical capacity to exercise can present challenges unimaginable in our youth.

As I've matured, I've discovered that remaining healthy in running requires compromise, careful planning and a lot of patience. Compromises have included fewer kilometres, daily stretching, more weight training, and more-informed choices of training courses.

This has been enough to keep my spluttering engine on the road, but not enough to prevent me from crashing along the way. In need of some heavy panel beating, and with my oil leaking, I recently received medical advice that I should quit running. My immediate response was, 'That's not an option.' Stupidity? Sure, but that's the way we runners are. Bloody minded. In the face of all obstacles, we remain defiant that we will run. We will always find a way to run.

If you are older, you should be wiser. Right? Yes, within limits. But I hate hearing those 'experts' whine on about how much we should rest just because we are older. Or how much we should cross train, just because we need to rest our legs. These are circular arguments of which I tire.

I want to run and only run. I don't want to cycle, or sink in an effort to swim. I don't want to become a poor excuse for a triathlete. I just want to race and run fast. I want to run consistently every day for that is the basis for success, in competition and in health. Nothing else matters. And nobody can tell me otherwise.

If you have read this far, you will understand that I am stubborn, and maybe even pigheaded (I like to think that I'm disciplined). But at my age, and maybe yours, we need to be resilient to keep on running, never mind competing. We need to out-think the signs of wear and tear. So, in our comebacks from injury, we start back easy with the acceptance that we may always have some level of discomfort in our legs.

But we are happy to be moving, no matter how slow. We avoid the hills and the road, we run on grass and on flat surfaces. We take an occasional foray into the hills and bush land to test our progress. We may even need a bit of physio. The secret is to move those limbs every day, in anticipation that we will return to our full range of physical mobility.

To recover from injury, if possible, I have always tried to maintain a daily run. You don't have to go far, but the routine of running is important. Sometimes when you have leg injuries it's not possible or advisable to run, and even your daily life can be affected. During these times, I use three lifestyle activity tests for measuring the progress of my recovery: the walking the dog (WTD) test, the mower (M) test and the walking down the stairs (WDS) test.

The WTD tests my ability to run in spurts at random as my Labrador drags me along the road, a form of easy fartlek if you like. The M tests my endurance to stay on my feet for two hours in the heat. The WDS test is a particularly brutal test of the mobility in my knees and stiffness in my Achilles tendons as I try to negotiate walking down the stairs into my backyard in a straightforward manner, not sideways like a crab.

When I can negotiate all three of these tests without significant pain or overcompensating for the injury, I know I am on my way back to full recovery. You may think I'm crazy, but I even record instances of WTD and M in my running diary as an indicator of how my injury may be affecting me.

Eventually that anticipation of a daily run is something that cannot be denied. Your psyche drives you to hobble out from regular periods of hibernation into the blaze of 'competition' at your local parkrun or a community event. Often it's too early to say you're fully recovered but enough to say you can give it a crack.

And therein lies the problem. Your mind is operating on an emotional level, no logic here. It is telling you mistruths about your ability to compete, and ultimately it drives you back into running oblivion, until the next time you come out of hibernation. And so it goes.

It's a funny thing, ageing, when you set your goals based on what you think you can physically achieve as you get older, and slower. You may even think you can run faster than those ahead of you in age, at their age, but you forget one thing: you have to get there first, in one piece. And that can take some doing. But whatever your journey, to cease running is not negotiable.

A Social Phenomenon

[Author's note: I penned this piece in 2015 for R4YL. It was written from the perspective of a competitive mature-aged club runner who had initially resisted the parkrun movement, happy to compete weekly in local Veterans/Masters track races. While parkruns were another avenue to 'compete' on some level, I saw them as a lesser event in this regard, with their much-vaunted support for social participation. So, it took me a while to engage with the parkrun community. Despite the furore of 2024 about the removal of its historical and cumulative statistics, and all that this means to the competitive among us, I think this piece rings true now, more than ever.]

Many years ago, a mature runner's options for competition were fairly restricted, split between Athletic Association events, Masters or Veterans organised events and annual fun runs. Of course, there were (and still are) other organisations such as the Victorian Marathon Club (VMC) and the Sydney Striders that catered less formally for a cohort of club runners of all ages.

However, competitive running was much more of a closed shop, with a reliance on rules and regulations and a strong demarcation between male and female participation. Older club runners would be found running tough at the back of the open fields with no recognition for their effort.

I was a club runner of the 1970s and '80s, and a sometimes fun runner. In my experience as a young club athlete, competition was front and centre, and club spirit was borne out of a need to compete. When I returned to distance running in 2006 I was struck by the pervasiveness of the recreational runner, with its decreased emphasis on hard-edged competition. The increase in women's participation was palpable. The emergence of parkruns in Newcastle and its environs triggered a landslide in community-based running and a web of social running clubs.

Apart from a loose but strong association with the Newcastle Veterans 'family' I have not re-engaged with the traditional athletics fraternity (whether NSW or Masters based). I have instead opted for the more-organic options available through our local community events and low-key Newcastle Veterans track races.

My experience seems to mirror that of many others. As far as I can see, mass participation in parkruns in the Region of Runners has translated into increased participation in other community-based events and running festivals (locally and interstate), and fringe disciplines, rather than the traditional track races and winter cross country events.

The social running club movement, at least in Newcastle, has sought to educate, promote, encourage and challenge its members to try new experiences, with the occasional foray into the 'traditional' – a toe in the ocean if you like, so it has all bases covered.

The parkruns are a kaleidoscope of backgrounds and relationships that cut across sporting endeavours and are spliced by the years of experience each participant brings to this community event. It's a welcoming environment, with no strings attached, apart from an underlying expectation that you volunteer to assist the event organiser from time to time.

You'll find yourself running side by side with trail and ultra-distance runners, hill climbers, triathletes, rowers, cyclists, football players, pram pushers and dog lovers, elite and plodder, men and women, young and old. Every week the kaleidoscope changes, bringing a new experience as participants opt in and out. Very different from my past, and admittedly very long ago, club running experience of racing the same guys, week in week out, no women allowed.

So, what is the attraction for mature runners? First and foremost, the community event enables participation at a low level. It is an easy avenue to starting exercise and looking after your health and wellbeing without any expectations about performance, or conforming to any hard and fast rules and regulations.

The community setting is a supportive environment, and a vehicle for gradual improvement in health and wellbeing. The community event is a meeting place for social inclusion. It is a vehicle for family, for volunteering, for forming strong friendships, and active engagement with others of all ages. Participants genuinely care. Even if you can't run because of injury, illness or personal circumstance, you can contribute social capital as a volunteer or supporter of local charitable events.

The informality of parkruns and the larger community events provide the perfect opportunity to compete or test yourself with anonymity as part of the crowd. It provides a focus for your week, a central commitment, an aspiration. And of course, if you are an elite mature-aged runner, it provides an opportunity to 'compete' hard and often, and maybe even 'win' the occasional race outright. So, if you are 'outside looking in', I encourage you to think seriously about joining the family.

The advent of social running clubs has created a plethora of pathways for mature runners to experience new endurance challenges. Often this forms the centrepiece for the next family holiday. Ultimately, this is its attraction. You've got it all, or at least a route to anything you want, but you don't have to commit. You can test and taste, repeatedly.

It's a social phenomenon. Why would you opt for anything else?

Ditch the Gear

Picture this. A bunched starting line, elite at the front, a gaggle of impatient racers pushing up from the back. There is a wave of outstretched arms, hands pressed against opposite wrists. Bent forward, waiting, waiting, then bang, a simultaneous beeping of watches and other timing devices. For simplicities sake, let's call them Casios, because that is my reference point from my younger running days. Remember them, those special watches of the 1970s with the ground-breaking facility for time and date?

Why would a racer be wearing a Casio? It's a puzzle to me. Oh, that's right, in this day and age with GPS, Garmins and other fancy devices, you can measure time and distance as you go. So what? Isn't there an official timing arrangement? I'm sure there must be.

Wearing a Casio in a race is the antithesis of racing. Actually, use of any technology during the race undermines self-confidence and the whole purpose of racing. It degrades the instinctive element. I sometimes have a circular debate with my running colleagues.

It goes like this;

Will wearing a Casio make you run any faster? Say you are racing slower than planned, will you speed up, or even be able to do this? Or is it just going to affect your mindset negatively for the rest of the race because you can't keep up with a pre-determined pace?

Say you are running faster than planned, will you slow down? Well, I don't think so, especially if you are having a good day. If you are feeling strong, like you'll hit a personal best or get that guy just in front, you'd want to go for it, wouldn't you? You have to grab those moments when they come.

Wearing a Casio in a race is an inhibitor, It will cause you to doubt yourself. Racing is combative. You need to be all there and all in, tactically aware, ready to respond. Sure, I know people have goals, based on time or pace. Or maybe you just want to get one up on that particular individual who always seems to beat you.

But the Casio douses the flame of competition and getting the best out of yourself. The race is the time to test those goals in a raw contest, competing. Don't be afraid to compete. That will bring you along, one way or another. As they say, the time will take care of itself, if you are true to yourself, your feelings, your senses, the contest.

I have never ever worn a Casio in a race. I just don't, not even in longer races like a marathon. I never did, never will. It's a distraction from your performance. I race by feel. If you are checking your watch regularly, then you are not focused on the other competitors, which is where your concentration should be. While you are preoccupied with your Casio, they are leaving you behind.

I had my best races solely by hanging on, embracing the feeling of hurt that inevitably comes and tracking my competitors in close quarters. It was heat-of-the-battle stuff, primordial, sharing the lead, passing and being passed, jockeying for position, digging deep, putting it in.

'What if I am out in front?' I can hear you say. 'Don't I need a Casio to pace myself?' I would argue that if you are in front, you've made the break, and you are probably the best in the field (at least on that day). Then, even moreso, you should rely on instinct and not a Casio to bring you home. Despite the huge digital clock on top of the lead car, it's your guts, your feel, your drive to hurt yourself, to run yourself out, that matters.

You are probably getting the drift that I dislike technology. Well, that's not true. I actually despise it. Earphones, heart-rate monitors and power meters, Strava, what could be worse? They just dull the experience of running. And come on, you can't actually be racing if you have one of those things plugged into your body.

I wouldn't even call them enablers, more like disablers. Technology just channels extraneous information into your being, taking you away from where you need to be, breeds more data to pore over and fret about. I make two exceptions. Heart rate monitors may have their place for runners, mature or young, who have particular medical conditions, and mobile phones can be essential items in some situations to ensure the safety of a lone runner.

But, for myself, now fit and healthy, I prefer to use the mother of all heart-rate monitors, my brain, to gauge pace and perceived exertion. Nature, feel, heightened sensory awareness, you can't go wrong.

Trust your body. Ditch the gear.

Join the Club? That's Not Entertainment Aka an Open Letter to Nobody

[Author's note: I wrote this piece many years ago. Although some may not agree with its sentiment, it reflected a concern about where things were heading at that time. Such sentiments were validated by contact I had with a British colleague, stalwart for want of a better word, who was lamenting the lack of depth in national distance running and the apparent demise of traditional AAA club networks that was affecting the development of elite performers. Seventeen years on it may be less relevant to today's competitive scene, but that is for the reader to judge.]

Since returning to distance running in 2006, I have noticed an increasing preoccupation with rejuvenating the athletics association club scenes. An underlying concern appears to be the promotion of club athletics as a major adult sport (which for the purpose of this article I define as conventional track running events, club cross country and road racing).

There seems to be an impression that somehow athletic club membership will increase just by tapping into the vast recreational participation pool that has developed over recent years; and will be assisted by promoting our sport as an entertainment product. But I don't think it's that easy, especially in middle distance and distance running.

This is nothing new. Sport is often confused as an entertainment product. In the 1800s and turn of the 20th century you could have called it showbiz or razzamatazz. In days gone by things were much simpler, but there was still commercialism in sport, sponsorship, money and betting, political and media influence.

However, our sport is so basic – after all, it's only about putting one foot in front of the other – that I think something has been missed in all of this. When it comes down to it, aren't we seeking a membership that want to compete hard, and for spectators of the elite competitors to appreciate the intrinsic worth of the contest and what went into it? How difficult can that be? And how complex do we need to make it?

The failure of our associations to compete successfully with other sports for athletic club membership may lie in the nature of our events, the level of individualism, and an inability to market this effectively to adults as their lifelong sport. We've always had plenty of children around, plenty of dropouts, young and middle-aged, and lots of unfulfilled potential. Ultimately, the club scene is a sport of hard-edged competition, not of participation per se. Sure, there is an obvious pathway from recreational participation to this level of competition, but it's not for the faint-hearted.

Colin Jackson, a former world recordholder for the 110m hurdles, describes this well: 'You line up alone against seven people who want, metaphorically, to destroy you. You want to come out on top to ice them. You win for yourself. Lose, and the pain and recriminations are for nobody else: just for you. And that's how I liked it.'[19]

Let's celebrate this fact, the hardness of it all, and make it our own, not hide it behind a perceived need for our sport to be an entertainment extravaganza promoting novelty events as a populist means of buying membership. The 'sell' should be purely about the contest and its intrinsic worth, warts and all, to witness as a spectator and be a part of as a competitor.

It's not glamour, it's grit. It's not about the team, it's about the self. It is all about the self and the discipline to commit to the training required to compete hard I mean really hard, And a true understanding of what it takes to compete, to become a champion.

My stance is basic – better to manage clear expectations of the club scene up-front than enable increased participation with an inevitable slow bleed in membership once the new aspirant finds how tough our sport really is.

And let's educate the spectators about the contest and the traditions of our sport, not acquiesce to overly commercial interests.

As a spectator I don't attend any sporting event, ours or others, wanting to be entertained. I want to see competitors, aspirants and champions in a hard-fought contest in events that I appreciate. Competing to win. All else is a distraction, an annoyance and something I can do without. I don't want the loud music, the screaming announcer, the fireworks and the dancing, or the novelty events.

It is very hard to get to the top of our sport. It requires a deliberate planned effort over many years, mixed with gut-wrenching quality sessions. We need to ensure we are not prostituting our sport in the name of increased membership that does not actually achieve a healthy elite.

It is important to our sports integrity to maintain its traditions in what our core constituency considers to be a lifelong commitment. Let's not mess with our traditions for the sake of a short-term revenue earner to attract spectators who will only ever have a cursory interest in our sport.

I come from a place when club athletics in NSW in the 1970s was a very poor cousin to just about everything else. But even at the 'scrubber' club level the overriding ethos was competition, to strive, to achieve, to compare yourself to the absolute best, no matter what your age. This does not sit nicely in an era of running mainly as a recreational past time where plaudits are rife for performances that are nowhere near what they could be.

Association club athletics has become a lifelong affair for the dedicated few. Many older runners still want to compete, race until they can't. Many stalwarts of our sport continue to contribute actively to the club scene through coaching and education, and in other capacities.

But it may take more than a few community-based invitation events to bring things along to where a lifelong commitment to our sporting contest becomes the norm, for competitor and spectator alike?

Or maybe I am out of step?

Personal Bests: The Grey of It All

For a mature runner, a personal best (PB) is a conundrum. Does a PB really exist? Purists of athletic endeavour say your PB distance-running performance is only achieved in your physical prime. Anything outside of that does not really count. Frank Horwill, a respected British coach and founder of the British Milers Club, identified the ages for peak performance of men as 25 for middle distances, 27 for 5km and 29 for 10km. Women were two years later at 27, 29 and 31 respectively.[20]

Ron Clarke expressed this sentiment nicely during an interview with Brian Lenton in 1979. Clarke agreed that Veteran athletics was inferior to open-type competition. He went on to say, 'It shouldn't be taken seriously in any way, shape or form … There's only one competition – open top athletics, when your best is pitted against the best from everywhere else and that's all there is to it. The rest is good fun as long as one doesn't take it seriously by saying "I'm the best in the world because I won an over-50 marathon in 2:35" or something.'[21]

Given the heights Clarke scaled, you can understand this viewpoint, and I have to admit that I don't disagree with such statements. My eyes glaze when I read about some textbook guru or personal trainer claiming how at 45, 50 or even 60 they have run their lifetime PBs and 'you can do it too' if you follow their program or join their squad. All part of the sell.

The only explanation for 'faster' times at older ages is late starts to running or not training effectively when younger. That's it. The science tells me, all things being equal, if your mental strength matches your physical capability, your absolute personal bests can only be achieved by/in your mid-20s.

When I look at my old training and racing diaries, I see a higher reward for training effort particularly between the ages of 22 and 24, and an ability to run at higher intensities in speed work and long runs with less comparative effort. In hindsight, I wasted some of these 'good' years with poor structure in my training, combined with a lack of discipline in balancing social commitments – an easy trap to fall into.

As a mature runner who experienced an 18-year hiatus before returning to distance running, I can't help but measure my current performance against my achievements when young. After all, it was me who ran that much faster, wasn't it? And I remain forever dissatisfied with how I perform now, despite any age grade 'frequent flyer point' calculations. My experience is different to many who have come new to distance running in middle age. For them it can be much more exciting as they see their PBs come down in large chunks, at least initially, as the training takes effect.

No matter what your age, the ability to 'hurt' yourself is the key to achieving a truly outstanding PB. These are situations where you can say with hand on heart, 'I gave it my all.' Of course, you can set PBs without 'hurting' yourself. It's not surprising how many take this easier approach to competition, satisfied purely with the joy of running. But you will never reach your true age racing potential adopting this stance.

For the racer, increased fitness builds the capacity to run harder and hurt yourself more and ultimately run faster. While the physiology of youth is the platform for great absolute performance, many of us can still run hard and fast if we so desire, despite the protestations of less-informed but well-meaning bystanders. Assuming you are in good health, the physiology of older age is unlikely to let the body damage itself.

I have noticed that getting older has resulted in a lack of consistency in race performance, despite what I consider to be high-level efforts. When racing weekly, while able to achieve good results virtually every time in my early 50s, in my late 50s I probably put up a strong performance about every fourth run. Maybe it has something to do with biorhythms, who knows? But it's a discernible trend for me, and I'd guess for many others.

Nothing beats the drag effect of open competition to achieve a PB. For the mature runner competing against others in the pack who are close to you in ability or slightly better makes it easier to 'hurt' yourself, if that is possible. However, Masters competition and age categories, combined with the age grade calculations, do much to support healthy, strong competition among older runners.

In particular, age grade calculations are useful to fuel your motivation by benchmarking current age performance against the actual performance of younger open competitors, your own PBs set at younger ages, and your age running peers, past and present.

Such calculations can also be a predictive tool to set race goals based on time. For instance, you can work out what your best PB set at age 25 equates to at your Masters age now, and set the latter as your race goal. Or you can estimate what the outright winner of an event may run and set your goal as your age grade equivalent of that time and see how close you can get.

You may be surprised that often the winners in age categories are running faster comparative times than outright winners, including against elite open winners. While this gives the well-performing mature runner a strong inner glow, maybe we could do a bit better than this and reward some of the Masters cohort for such supreme efforts with significant prize money. I can understand a reluctance to do so, because we don't want to take away from the outright winner's achievement. God forbid. However, the age grade calculation tools have become more reliable over time as a valid means of age-to-age comparison.

At a minimum, at major events like running festivals, I'd like to see a second set of official results published purely on age grade performances. Surely our age demographics demand it as Grey Power flexes its running legs over the next few decades.

As well as encouraging runners of all ages, maybe it would provide some extra motivation for our elite runners to achieve greater performance? After all, what 25-year-old wants to be beaten by a 65-year-old, no matter what the context? Pie in the sky some will say, but maybe it's legitimate food for thought for race event organisers?

Remember, from little things big things grow.

Weights for Weights' Sake

Some of us have used weights casually throughout our running careers without really understanding their benefits. Others have never used weights, viewing strength training as non-essential for successful distance running.

There is a common view that strength training can develop unwanted muscle that takes more energy to carry, adversely affecting our ability to run fast. However, other literature disagrees with this view.[22] Some even contend that, when used on a limited basis, heavier weights can have a positive effect on the development of muscle power, increasing our capacity to resist fatigue in endurance events, and that bulking up only occurs through taking in excess calories, lifting 4-5 times per week and having adequate rest from catabolic activities such as running.[23]

A complicating factor for mature runners is the reduction in muscle mass that accompanies increased age. Muscle mass declines at a rate of 8 percent every 10 years from the ages of 25-30. There is a concurrent loss of bone mass at a rate of 1 percent a year from age 35.[24] The resulting loss of muscle strength can affect the older person's quality of life and increase the risk of injury. It therefore seems to make sense to conduct year-round strength training to aid running performance and reduce the risk of injury from weak muscles and fragile bones.

It has long been argued that weight training improves running economy, increases the capacity to exercise to exhaustion, improves neuromuscular coordination and anaerobic performance. Upper body development can also improve running posture, respiratory efficiency and resistance to arm fatigue over longer distances. [25 26 27 28]

Goater and Melvin identify upper body strength as important to running fast. In recommending a range of strength regimes, including light weights, they state, 'Your arms act as your accelerator pedal and your legs will never be able to go faster than your arms.'[29]

With increased age, I have gravitated to heavier free weights (as a proportion of my body weight and in real terms) for upper body development to provide a more substantial improvement in my distance running. The challenge of lifting heavy weights is hard to describe. I find it even more basic than running, requiring a moment in time when I am pitting my innate strength against the bar. The sensation after these sessions is 'mellow with a sting', and the power I feel in my running defies belief.

Percy Cerutty shows how it's done in deadlifts, one of the best all-round lifts to minimise injury. Credit: *Be Fit! or Be Damned!*

Of course, mature runners have to be careful lifting weights, particularly as we approach 60 and beyond. We have particular health risks that are more acute and need to be managed. These include a higher propensity towards osteoporosis, more-tender joints, stiffer tendons and, for some, muscles significantly atrophied. Medical clearance is therefore advisable for those who have not previously used weights.

It may also be safer for some mature runners to use machines rather than free weights or to mix their strength training with circuit training and power-development exercises. To ensure correct technique, it is a good idea to lift weights in a controlled environment, like a gym, while under strict supervision. At the very least, always use a spotter if using free weights.

The beauty of heavy weights is that you can achieve optimal benefit from a short, sharp session. However, it is prudent to research and seek advice about the lift types that will meet your specific needs in muscular development. I tend to focus on curls, bench press, vertical rows and pull-ups. I find that two sessions a week are enough to support a program of progressive adaptation that helps my running. More recently, I have included deadlifts as a whole-of-body strength exercise.

'Heavy' is a relative term, varying by individual and depending on age, gender, and base muscular strength. For instance, at 74kg and 56 years of age, I could bench press three sets of 3 x 64kg as a challenging target, having started at three sets of 6 x 45kg some months earlier. Over time I was able to achieve a one-rep maximum bench press of 70kg. At the time of writing, aged 65, I am rebuilding and I can just manage three sets of 3 x 63kg. To a young man in his early 20s, it would be laughable to describe my lifts as heavy.

As with interval training, I find my tolerance for weight training can be greatly affected by other physical activity outside my normal exercise routine. I therefore like to ensure I am fully rested to get the best out of my weight sessions. The training adaptation effect can be controlled by varying the weight of the lift, the number of repetitions, the number of sets and the duration of rest intervals.

In terms of the latter, especially when lifting 'heavy' weights, I do not time my rest intervals, only attempting another set when I feel psychologically and physically ready. Despite this, I am sometimes unable to manage the same number of reps in my last set as my first, due to fatigue.

While my preference is to lift 'heavy' weights and until recently limiting my efforts to upper body development, I believe any form of strength training for the whole body (including lighter weights) is essential for the wellbeing and performance of mature distance runners.

The benefits of strength training as we continue to age cannot be denied. For us, it ultimately becomes a case of weights for health's sake, if nothing else.

Solitary Man: A Vignette

Tomorrow everything will be different.

Frank did his best problem solving during his evening runs. Sometimes he would work an all-nighter, taking a break with a quick run between his daily business commitments and a late evening shift. The run gave him the space to deconstruct and reconstruct the issues of the day. The run always gave him something.

Frank had a sporting past of sorts. Plenty of unfulfilled potential. He loved the distance running game. To him it was all about the competition and the reliance on self that it taught. Racing was a basic truth, a law of nature – what you put in you got back. A bit like life is supposed to be, but isn't.

Here, near Newcastle, Australia, there wasn't a race tomorrow, so he took the opportunity to explore the local area with a longer-than-normal training jaunt. It was one of those crisp-dry evenings that demanded minimal clothing, and Frank happily obliged. He didn't care who saw him, never felt embarrassed. *Their issue not mine* was his mantra. Often required to travel, Frank carried his kit with him so he could have a run wherever he happened to be. It was part of his life routine of work, running, bed. All he needed was shorts and shoes, not even a T-shirt most of the year, because it was so bloody hot.

Approaching dusk, barrelling through the coastal bushland was exhilarating. The dirt was easy on his legs and the intermittent shade of the gum trees gave relief from a sapping sun that thrived on daylight saving. The salt air pushed firmly on to his bare chest, the sweet aroma of eucalyptus seeping into his nostrils. Sweat trickled through his threadbare shorts down his legs to well-worn Nike trainers. The inevitable squelch arrived 30 minutes in.

He was mulling over what to say to his daughter, when seconds later he found himself face down on the ground. Free-wheeling through rough terrain, caught unawares, Frank had stubbed his toe and plunged head-first into the coastal scrub. It was a hell of a spectacle, an act that would take a circus clown years to perfect, and Frank did it intuitively, although not as gracefully as he would have liked.

Stunned, he lay moaning a shallow riff until his breathing stabilised. He came around slowly, gagging and hacking red-brown muck, feeling for arms and legs that had been ripped by hard earth. Burning pain shot through jarred wrists.

As the brain fog lifted, Frank was startled by a rustling sound. With a quiet snuffle and muffled grunt, a brown ball of spines appeared from a nearby thicket. It brushed past Frank's face like he didn't exist. A river of expletives sprayed from Frank's lips, echoing off the large bush rock surrounds, as the creature waddled away, oblivious to Frank's situation.

In his own time Frank clawed himself upright, grappling with thick undergrowth and wincing as native brambles and briar attacked his battered limbs. Self-conscious, Frank glanced around to check for onlookers.

Close call, he thought, seeing the sheer cliff before him as he staggered off, sorry for himself. The blood on his hands and elbows was drying, his knees a mix of cuts and abrasions.

Looks worse than it is, thought Frank, convincing himself. Now back into full stride, shorts caked in grime, knees still leaking, the limp was subsiding.

\#

Danielle was waiting on the front verandah of their cabin. A cooling breeze had struck up, salt landing on everything in its path.

'Quite a sight, I must say,' said Danielle dryly, from under her baseball cap. 'What have you done to yourself? Don't tell me, fall over again?'

'What does it look like?' said Frank, tired and worse for wear. 'Tripped over a fucking echidna, that's what.'

She stared at him with a combination of mock surprise and admiration. *Dad will never stop running,* thought Danielle, *run 'til he drops.*

'You're kidding,' said Danielle. 'That's a new one,' blue eyes sparkling. 'Poor bloody echidna. Did it survive? You didn't land on it, did you?'

Frank shot back a filthy glance. 'Dani, don't take the piss, I've told you what happened. Now leave it alone. I just want to get cleaned up.'

Danielle had come along for the ride to look out for her old man. Of course, she didn't tell him that was the reason. As young daughters sometimes do, she lied to her father, but it was only a white lie. Danielle told Frank she needed a break from her job, and his business trip to Newcastle would give her the perfect opportunity to relax and spend more time with him. Fathers like hearing such stuff from their daughters, and who can blame them When it came to Dani, Frank was a sop like most dads.

Frank stumbled through the doorway, knees and hands stinging. He was stiffening up as his body cooled down.

'Give me a look at your hip,' said Danielle, noticing his discomfort.

Frank sat down gingerly on the rock-hard divan. 'Okay girl, just let me rest for a bit. I'll be all right in a tick,' he said with a grimace as he stretched his legs to ease the tightness. He had runner's legs, knobbly knees and big calves.

Danielle sidled up to her father and tugged at his shorts. 'Can't you get a better pair?' she quipped. 'Guess Mum's right. She always says you run around the streets half naked, that you're an embarrassment.'

Frank smiled, 'I don't care what your mother says, kid. We have an understanding of sorts. I run, and she lets me, that's all that matters.'

'Well, if you keep having these falls, Dad, the decision will be made for you. Not by me, or Mum, but by your own body. It's not unusual to lose your sense of balance as you get older. Maybe you just need to ease up on the running.'

He knew she was right, although he would never admit it. *I will run, always run. What do the quacks know? Nuthin'*, he thought.

Banter finished, message delivered, Danielle returned her attention to Frank's hip, 'Lucky you've only bruised it, but you've given it a good whack. A bit more to come out yet I'd say. What if you break something next time?'

Frank snapped back, 'Not going to happen, kiddo. Don't worry about me. I'll get myself into the bath. Then we can have a chat, out on the verandah if you like. Cold beer would go down a treat. How about that?'

Frank lurched from the divan towards the bathroom. Danielle knew he wouldn't want her help as she watched him carry his aches and pains to the tub.

'Sure, Dad, I'm up for a chat, but let's see how you feel.'

Shortly after, she heard the oohs and aahs as her father entered the water. She laughed to herself as Frank lowered himself and sank into the business of a good soak.

#

Frank returned 40 minutes later in shorts and singlet, Victoria Bitter in hand. Refreshed, he found Danielle crashed out on the divan. She lay curled up in a bunch of arms and legs.

He sat at her feet, waiting for her to stir. He was thinking all those things that fathers think about their daughters, the good and the bad, but mostly the good.

Simply put, Danielle is an accomplished, independent woman, who knows her own mind. There is no other way to describe her. Even as a little girl she was defiant, not in an objectionable way, but in a manner that excited her mother and I that she would be able to make her own way in life. It was part of our family's story, told and retold umpteen times. When three-year-old Dani stomped her feet and threw her determination back up the hallway at us: I'll never forget those words: 'This is my life and I'll do what I want to do.'

Every so often a stream of air flew from her mouth as a whistling nearly-snore.

Loves her sleep does Dani.

He had wanted Danielle's advice tonight, to talk through his situation, to break it down. It was all getting a bit much, his thoughts overwhelming logic with emotion. Frank needed honesty, and he knew she would give it to him in spades.

He sighed as he realised that Danielle was done for the night.

I guess it's not going to happen tonight. Not now, not ever.

He pulled the blanket over his daughter with a father's tenderness many times unseen.

Head in hands, shaking uncontrollably, the angst welled up from the pit of his stomach and gushed through his lungs. He caught himself just enough to prevent an absolute flood. The doctor's phone call was still raw, messing with his head. That talk about mortality was not something he wanted to hear as he recalled an appalling bedside manner.

Tomorrow is coming quicker than I anticipated.

In an effort to calm himself, Frank paced the room. His whole being craved tranquillity, the oneness that only solitude can deliver. He stopped abruptly as he came to his decision.

Maybe it's better this way.

As he placed the half-empty can on the kitchen table, the rugged coastal landscape beckoned. Standing in the cabin doorway, he took one last look at his daughter.

At least I've done one thing right in my life.

Ocean winds swirling, he jammed on his Nikes.

Then he was gone.

Feet: A Cautionary Tale

How often do you think about your feet? You really should pay them some attention. Older feet can stay 'young' if treated with the care they need.

There is no right or wrong when it comes to your feet and their house, the shoe. Everyone is different. However, as my experience shows, your feet are precious things and you mess with them at your peril. It took 40 years of unintentional trial and error to get to where I am now: on the way to being injury free, at least in the feet!!

Did you know that your feet change with ageing? This is a natural process, not affected in the slightest by running, it happens to everyone, runner and non-runner. But such changes will need to be accommodated in your future decision making about footwear. The major changes are widening and lengthening of your feet, a loss of padding under-foot that affects your power, stiffness that affects mobility in foot and ankle, a loss of balance, and a flattening of foot caused by very mild settling of the arches. 'The most common foot complaints by older adults are toenail and skin problems, calluses or corns, swelling, bunions and arthritis.'[30]

And women are a special case, typically with much shorter feet than men, possibly the result of an evolutionary process, or simply a function of their smaller body size? One informal study even found that women's feet were shorter than their body size would predict when compared to men.[31] Dainty feet that require some hardening I say, for the power of speed comes from your feet!

Every day we make intuitive decisions about our feet and footwear that can affect our ability to run or perform to our best. Light shoes or heavy? Flats or spikes? Socks or no socks? Burst that blood blister or leave it alone? Orthotics or not? Heel and/or arch support, or not? Tape the feet or risk the blisters? Vaseline or not? Hard sole or soft sole? These decisions can be affected by the context. Is it a race or just training we are talking about? It's easy to make a rash decision when about to race, especially if you are searching for that edge that will give you the win or could result in your best performance. It is also easy to make poor long-term decisions because of a personal bias, rather than seeking professional advice and using an objective analysis of your own biomechanics, lower leg strengths and weaknesses.

Surprisingly, during my fifties I graduated to a more minimalist, but not too extreme, approach for training shoes. Some contend that mature runners may adapt to shoe changes more slowly than younger runners, given their years of ingrained footfall. And that a change from heel and mid foot strike to the fore foot strike of barefoot running or minimalist shoes can be problematic, bringing with it a higher risk of lower leg injury, such as fractures.[32] Others warn that a lack of stability from light weight training shoes may only suit a slight runner who does not suffer pronation problems.[33] Certainly, for mature runners, caution is required in managing this transition. Luckily for me, while heavier than many, I tend to mid/fore foot strike and have no obvious pronation issues.

But taking that step to run barefoot is a totally different proposition. I have run barefoot in a light five kilometres here or there on a grass oval; or during a short cool down on a beautifully manicured soccer pitch. Nothing beats that feeling of release for your feet. These short forays into barefoot running have served to identify a lack of strength in some areas of my feet and lower legs. All things considered I'm not prepared to risk training totally unshod. And I'm not sure that the time taken to adapt is worth the effort for the average older athlete. Though Masters record breaker Keith Bateman has been a proponent of barefoot running, so there must be something to it?

The question of orthotics is an interesting one. The experts will tell you that wearing orthotics is not a sign of weakness. The American running doctor of the 1970s, Steven I. Subotnick DPM, MS provides timeless advice: '..the orthotic does not support the foot; it merely allows the foot to get into proper positions so the muscles can do their job in aligning the joints, and the bony architecture of the foot can do its job in actually supporting the body weight.....because there is better phasic activity and muscle function, the lower extremities become stronger.'[34]

At the age of 50 during a local Veterans track race I had to stop after three laps and couldn't put my foot to the ground, an early indication of plantar fasciitis, so I was told. I was fitted with some orthotics and after three days of rest, I was able to resume running with no ill effects. However, I resented my reliance on these 'supports', as a vulnerability that came with ageing. Foolishly, perhaps, three years later I ceased wearing orthotics. Within two months, I had aggravated an Achilles tendon injury that I had been nursing throughout my career.

While I did not revert to orthotics again, I experienced significant disruption to my running during the next four years. With some guidance from allied health professionals, I gradually transitioned to a light-weight minimalist shoe, of sorts (I wear flat soft-soled training and racing shoes with no heel or arch support). Of necessity this included a commitment to a heavy rehab program concentrating on strengthening my core and my knees, Achilles tendon and ankles. The rehab program included the use of isometric calf raisers. This exercise provided immediate pain relief for my Achilles tendon condition, until then unachievable.

Another critical factor to my successful transition was wearing flat business shoes at work with no heels whatsoever. It took me a while to figure out just how much my heeled shoe was aggravating my Achilles tendon. Notably, in everyday life, practically year around, I am barefoot, an informal strengthening strategy for the feet and lower leg. At least that's the way I see it.

Now in my mid-sixties, I have actually noticed a splaying of the feet, they are wider than before, my underfoot is thinner, my toes are a mess and my nails no better. But the only adjustments I've had to make is a more padded sole, still with no arch support, and an intermittent use of orthotics to save my metatarsals.

So, when it comes to footwear, think carefully. If things are working for you my advice is don't fool with it. If things are not, only tinker at the edge of that continuum between barefoot and orthotic (with professional guidance) until you find the right fit for you, for your age.

A Man for All Ages

I love Arthur Lydiard's teachings. His revolutionary ideas about distance running ring in my ears even now, years after the achievements of Snell, Baillie, Halberg, and Magee. Lydiard truly was a distance running and fitness guru. While Lydiard influenced many great runners and coaches, by all reports he was a man for the people, providing encouragement to runners of all abilities. Well before his time, in the early 1960s Lydiard promoted jogging and distance running for the middle aged and older person as a means of improving health and supporting cardiac rehabilitation.[35]

Lydiard's basic philosophy is epitomized by his own words in *Run to the Top* first published in 1962: 'Fit men develop a pride in themselves that transcends the moderate effort they are required to make to maintain that fitness. Many of my school of runners now don't run in the hope that they will win races. They run because they want to stay fit in later life and because they enjoy the social atmosphere and freedom of body and spirit experienced in bush runs, road runs, and jogs along the beaches.'[36]

The essence of Lydiard's system can be described as 'Your performance level is really governed by your aerobic capacity and your anaerobic capacity is limited in its extent.'[37] There has been much debate, and some misunderstandings, about Lydiard's teachings. My view is the simplicity of his message just confused people. We tend to look for complexity where it doesn't exist. Lydiard's system was distilled from trial and error over many years, with himself as the guinea pig. It was raw truth, borne of real sweat and effort, and undeniable in its positive honing of human physiology.

For competitive athletes, a Lydiard program is premised on peaking for a major event. I believe in peaking but never really had a go at it. That was more about my lack of discipline than any issue with Lydiard's approach. These days a Lydiard program is often 'adapted' in an abridged format or different parts of the system accentuated to the perceived strength of the individual athlete – sometimes at the expense of a supreme achievement if it had been implemented in its purest form.

Arthur Lydiard in full flight winning a mile race at Sarawia Park, Newmarket, likely during late 1940s. Credit: *Arthur Lydiard: Master Coach.*

The primary phases of Lydiard's system are conditioning of 100 miles per week at high aerobic effort for up to six months (plus supplementary morning jogs), a six weeks speed phase including hill work, four to five weeks of hard anaerobic track work and time trials, culminating with a sharpening phase of two weeks.[38][39]

If healthy, an elite athlete in their forties may be able to follow a similar Lydiard program to a younger athlete. And a healthy 40 year old is physiologically and muscularly strong enough to benefit from such a program. However, into the next two decades I accept that an amended Lydiard program is required to mitigate the risk of injury as we age. The following observations are worth consideration for a mature competitive athlete:

Conditioning - instead of 100 miles pw (160km), run 100kmpw. Only run once per day without supplementary morning jogs. Abide strictly to alternate hard day/2 days easier, rather than one for one. Its notable that Lydiard also promoted alternating between hilly courses and flat, long and short in developing a conditioning program.[40]

Lydiard has stated it is more economical to perform the bulk of conditioning on the roads.[41] And this is true. However, running on varied surfaces can assist in retaining a sense of spatial balance as part of human movement, something that can diminish with age.

Hill Circuits - Lydiard describes this phase as exacting and initially difficult, requiring dogged perseverance. 'Always bear in mind that the wise only train according to their age, physical condition and their capacity to exercise. They learn quickly about themselves and train by that knowledge, increasing volume and intensity of work only when they feel their condition is improving.'[42]

Hill work develops power and flexibility in the legs, increasing the capacity for speed work.[43] Instead of performing bounding on short sharp hills, compromise by performing the bulk of your reps over longer less acute gradients. Remember to support this adaptation phase with exercises that promote suppleness.

While Lydiard included hill work as resistance training and did not advocate weight training, this would not be enough to forestall the loss of muscle a mature person experiences. So other resistance exercises apart from hill work remain a real consideration.

Anaerobic Phase - Lydiard describes a suite of training methods (primarily on the track) to develop anaerobic capacity such as paarlauf training, fartlek, time trials, repetitions, sharpeners and sprint training.[44] The mature runner may be best advised to use 'softer' methods such as fartlek that underlies effort and feel to optimize the outcomes of this phase without risking over-exertion.

There is much about the Lydiard system to like for the mature. This includes his recommendation that you should train by time rather than distance as you adapt to increased mileage, that adaptation to all phases of his system will occur if patient, and that long runs at high aerobic effort are steady and even, leaving the athlete 'pleasantly tired' but with something in reserve.[45]

A short precis such as this cannot do justice to the detailed information Lydiard and his disciples have provided that underpins this simplest of systems. His advice is timeless and his writings are priceless. If you have not read Lydiard's work you are not truly educated in the ways of middle and distance running. Even if you have, I suggest you may need to read them again (and again) to truly understand his messages.

The only slight reservation I have about using Lydiard principles is will the time invested in conditioning create a training effect that can offset the reductions in racing performance caused by ageing? But rest assured I intend on using my Soft Quality Program to finally transition to a Lydiard System in my mid-sixties.

As Lydiard was fond of saying, the proof is in the pudding.

Not Whinging, Just Sayin'

I often pine for the good old days when life seemed so much simpler, running was basic, competition seemed harder and the club runner was paramount. But think of this, sixty years ago, in the early to middish 1960s:

There were no garmins

There were no lycra sports clothing or compression garments

There were no household treadmills

There were no mass-produced orthotics

There was no bottled water, commercially sold

There were no sports gels

There were no sports drinks

There were no mass-produced multi vitamins

There were no sports doctors for the people

There was no industry of personal trainers

There were no women long distance runners

There were no mixed races

There were no fun runs or community-based running festivals

There were no instant race results published on the net

There were no synthetic tracks

There were no Masters competitions or Masters clubs

There was no Little Athletics

There was no official prize money for amateurs

There was no Australian Institute of Sport

There were no pace makers in elite races

Fully automatic timing had not been officially sanctioned

Triathlons did not exist

Mass participation did not exist

There was no Australian Team competing in the International Cross Country Championships

There was no African world dominance

But:

There were handheld stop watches

There were printed results sheets, sometimes roneo'd or typed, and you got them in the mail

There was a limited range of running shoes

There were cinders and grass tracks

There were club runners who ran cross-country, road and track races

There were a few joggers

There were weekly interclub track races in the burning sun

There were masseuses and rub-downs

There were amateur coaches

There were 'real runners' who trained hard and raced tough

There was 'shamateurism'

There was a professional runners league that didn't race the amateurs

If you were lucky, there were water stations at every 5km of a marathon

There were old guys hanging on for grim death at the back of the pack in weekly winter club events

There was the Australian Harrier published on a shoe string

There was a pre-eminent South Australian journal called Modern Athlete and Coach

There was the Victorian Marathon Club and its quarterly newsletter.

Don't ask me why, but reflecting on this era, at home and abroad, the following images are etched in my mind:

Sandgroper, Jim Langford, beating Ron Clarke in the 1965 Australian Cross Country Championships;

John Farrington competing in the relative anonymity of Australia, having won the 1963 Junior International Cross Country Championships;

Merry Lepper setting an unofficial world best women's marathon time of 3:37:07 in the 1963 Culver City marathon, despite being harangued by race officials;

Peter Buniak establishing the groundwork for Jerome Drayton;

Ron Clarke in his heyday, breaking 13 minutes for 3 miles;

Kip Keino at the vanguard of an African explosion, throwing his cap down with a lap to go;

Peter Snell beaten by Bill Crothers at Toronto in 1965, vanquished but magnanimous in defeat;

Hard men like Hill, Bullivant, Fowler, Turner, Johnston, Hogan, Freary, Batty, Heatley, Hyman, Kilby, and the North brothers racing tough and often barefoot in the British AAAs 6 miles Championships;

Ralph Doubell training under Franz Stampfl at Melbourne University, on his way to Olympic gold;

Fred Lester, slouch hat on head and megaphone in hand, barking out instructions in his distinctive European accent on VMC race day; and

Colin Smith, Alan Sillitoe's antihero in *The Loneliness of the Long Distance Runner*, deliberately stopping short of the finish line in a defiant gesture towards the school establishment.

So, were things better in the early sixties? Well, I'm not whinging, but I'm just sayin I think they probably were, for men anyway (sadly this was not an era that welcomed women). Yeah, I know I am biased, because the sixties were the stories of my running youth, told in the 1970s, and what I thrived on for inspiration and motivation. It was an era romanticised by the 'old boys', the great racers eulogised in books, magazines and any old film clips I could get my hands on.

It was an era when distance runners worked for a living and achieved great things despite the social system they trained and raced within. When men and women distance runners faced significant challenges with dismal levels of support external to their families. Where instant gratification through social media and other technology tools wasn't available or would not have been sought even if possible. When patience, persistence and hard graft were rewarded. When people raced each other regularly to improve their performances and bring everyone else along. When marathon mania hadn't hit the general populace. And when the track times achieved on grass and cinders were in many ways far superior to the achievements of our modern-day racers, who have fast times handed to them on a plate with financial stipends, synthetic surfaces and pace makers.

Then again, maybe I'm only seeing what I want to see, and really it wasn't all that different back then? Just the start of a slow burn to what we have now, for better or worse. And in fifty years' time what will they be saying about the current era? I can only imagine, for while some of you may be here I will not.

A Matter of Balance

Recently I have been reading about proprioception, the scientific word for your brain's ability to direct your body to sure footing. Vonhof describes it as a sixth sense, a means of making adjustments mid stride to the terrain beneath you.[46] As we get older our ability to exercise a high degree of proprioception can diminish unless we make a conscious effort to strengthen critical parts of our leg such as the ankle and knees.

Joyce Smith, British distance running icon in Open and Masters competition, stopped running at age 74 because of concerns about falling. As she said 'as you get older … you don't pick up your feet so much'. Joyce translated to gym work and static cycling as a safer option to maintain a level of fitness in her mature years.[47]

I thought about this for a fleeting moment when I was careering through coastal bush tracks, having tripped over a protruding tree root, and heading towards a sheer cliff. Fortunately, I managed to crash into some side bushes, falling prostrate on my back like a stunned mullet. Having had a close call my wife's words caused me to take stock: 'what if you fall over in Glenrock Reserve and I don't know where you are?' Lesson learnt. I had to do something about it.

Proprioception can be improved by running regularly on soft and uneven ground. However, this needs to be in a safe environment. Talking from experience, your sixties is when the body can really start to fall apart if given half a chance, and certainly balance can be off if you do not work at it. To get a sense of where you sit in this matter of balance try the following simple exercises:

- Stand on one foot for 30 seconds, each leg 10 times.

- Try an arabesque bending forward and coming back up as ballerinas do but without leaning on a support bar. 10 reps on each leg.

- Lower yourself on one leg with back straight, onto a bench or soft seat – don't let yourself fall – control the lowering with your leg muscles. 10 reps on each leg.

If you can only do one rep, or can't do any, don't be disheartened, that was my experience. I found the third exercise the most difficult. My physiotherapist had to practically badger me into doing the exercise after many failed attempts at home. But with concentration and focus you will soon be able to do them all with ease. It just requires some neurological re-wiring that occurs by repeated attempts, and ultimately it will result in a more confident and intuitive runner.

It is reported that use of a wobble or rocker board can be beneficial in the rehabilitation of an injured ankle. If done when fatigued (after the end of a workout) balancing for up to 30 seconds may assist the required neurological adaptation to prevent future injury. Some recommend that once you can do it for 30 seconds you should try it with your eyes closed.[48] Of course, if you are embarking on such a rehab regime advice from a medical practitioner or allied health professional should be sought.

A confident balanced older athlete is better prepared to try different sports. The World Masters Games provides such an opportunity. With an element of fun chucked in for good measure. While we have a tendency to compete in pursuits that are familiar to us, the Games provides' an avenue to explore other disciplines.

I have noticed many athletes becoming multi-disciplinarian as they get older, extending into ultras, triathlons, and cycling. The Games bring all of the various sports together in one major event as a means to try new things, and can provide an incentive for an adventurous cross over to other disciplines, four years or more in the making.

It is not surprising that many stalwarts of renowned individual pursuits such as athletics experiment in team sports the Games affords. This level of cross over is testament to the ability of the Games to support participation and fun as a sought-after adjunct to serious competition. After all we need to have fun.

It's all a matter of balance.

Lamentations of an Older Don't Wanna-Be Marathoner

The marathon scares me. It demands respect but gets so little in return. Contemporary attitudes' of 'near enough is good enough' and 'just finishing is a great accomplishment' are hard for me to fathom. I understand the marathon's allure but not the under-estimation of the preparation required, and the promotion of minimalist programs just to get you through. The thing is, even now at 65 years of age, if I was to enter a marathon, I'd want to beat it, not just run it.

Now let me say that I am no elitist. I do understand and appreciate the sense of achievement that can arise from finishing a marathon. It's no mean feat, especially for a mature person who is often faced with a myriad of issues just to get to the starting line. However, I'm not one to use age as an excuse for accepting less than my best. Respect yourself I say, and of course respect the distance, but why not give yourself every opportunity to do your best?

I raced a handful of marathons but nothing to write home about. My last marathon was in 1988, age 29, and I still bear the emotional scars of a potentially good performance gone awry. While my marathon experience was 36 years ago, I remember with clarity my various attempts at running marathons. The jabbing pains in my hamstrings towards the end, the squelch in my shoes as the sweat envelopes my feet, the sharp ache in my right elbow as I wiped my brow, the slow drain of life force from 32 kilometres onwards, the sucking of sponges, the blisters, the chafing and the glazed look in the eyes of those around me as they bunker down for the last 10 kilometres. Of concern to me, more recently these images have seeped into my psyche pulling me towards a supposedly inevitable outcome: that I will run a marathon again.

Be warned, I have been told that while you can achieve outstanding race results in the half marathon by training primarily for 10 kilometres, you cannot achieve a great marathon performance solely on the back of a half marathon training program. The marathon is a totally different animal. I laugh when I think about my post-race experience after one Canberra Nike Marathon event – hold up on a toilet in a friend's home, not able to move for half an hour because of severe cramping in my legs and God knows where else. And that was when I was young and did some reasonable preparation! I can't imagine the state I'd be in if I tried one now.

To train for a marathon when you are older is a complicated thing. We are ageing, it never stops, and the contemporary advice is for a mature person to focus on quality over quantity to achieve high-level distance running performances. And I think that it is right to maintain high quality training of some description for the marathon, but not at the total expense of the base. No matter what your age, to **race** a marathon comfortably you just gotta put in the miles, there ain't no way around it, despite what some fitness gurus may say. But while volume is a given, it just won't cut it on its own.

To find the appropriate dose of quality for the marathon I suggest us oldies walk a finer tight rope than those much younger. I also suggest that the 'Just Forty' brigade are much like their younger counterparts, able to maintain very high levels of absolute performance, even if their training regime is not quite optimal, with a heavier leaning towards quantity. But for those approaching 50 and beyond it's a case of finding the ideal quality ingredient that will improve marathon performance and mitigate the ageing effect – and mix it with traditionally accepted dosages of quantity. Is there such a thing? I'd like to think so, but I'm not going to find out by running slow.

Unfortunately, many running programs tend to be written with little tailoring of advice for mature athletes. What we need is a Champion of the Elderly willing to engage in personal experimentation of 'Lydiardesque' proportions. The end game is to identify and promulgate the optimal type and level of quality in the training programs of mature athletes to achieve their best marathon performance. I could be wrong, but I don't believe this has been done as any form of rigorous longitudinal research.

For me the lure of the marathon was quickly eradicated when I bumped into a young runner during a weekend run through coastal bush land. He advised me that he was training for a 60 kilometres race, did an occasional parkrun but preferred the grinding pain of ultras to the acute pain of running fast over shorter distances, 10 kilometres and under. I was dumbstruck. Oh, I thought, what I would give to have the benefit of his youth to absolutely smash myself at top speed again.

And with that exchange came my epiphany: I don't need to run another marathon, what I need is to get it out of my mind. While I remain in awe of the mature ultra-distance runner, I am quite happy for my longest distance racing experience to be capped at the marathon, as a past and not future experience, at least until I run my next marathon!!

The Ultimate Free Form

Fartlek is a staple part of many runner's programs, elite and scrubber alike, but executed in many different forms. It is an ideal type of training for a mature runner wanting to remain competitive on some level. It's the ultimate free form of quality running if you are willing to open your heart to its benefits. The mistake many of us make is to try and provide structure around something that is supposed to be speed play, 'play' being the operative word. Goater & Melvin describe unstructured fartlek as a very effective way to transition to faster running and improved performance, that should be an integral part of every runner's program.[49]

The beauty of fartlek for a mature person is it allows us to include an additional quality session for the fortnight; where otherwise we may not. Typically, it involves a period of 'working into it', building speed and effort, until you have a sense of how you may be feeling. If done honestly, it can result in a great speed endurance session. You will be surprised at how hard you will push yourself based purely on your inner drive.

Fartlek is viewed by some as the poor cousin to interval training and I'm not sure why, because fartlek can be highly intensive. Maybe it's an old-world concept no longer fit for purpose to high tech modern coaching systems? Anyway, to be an effective session I find it relies on you running alone, and not being influenced by someone else's pace. It is not a social exercise. It is about being in tune with your own body and responding to your senses. You control how you respond: easy, medium or hard effort; slow, steady or fast pace; short recovery breaks or long, decelerating or ramping it up; and inevitably your senses are heightened by your choice of natural surroundings.

Fartlek in its purest form is about throwing structure out the window and truly running on instinct. This means not measuring the distance, not knowing when your current burst of speed is going to end or when the next one will start, not using pre-determined active rest breaks between surges, not knowing how many surges you will do in a session, not using set landmarks to gauge effort, just running at speed until you feel you need to stop for that level of effort then repeating a surge some time else over a distance you haven't thought of until you are in the moment and about to set off on the next surge. Sounds erratic, I know, but that's its attraction.

Gunder Hagg of Sweden was a beautiful stylist and a proponent of fartlek. He was the first to break 14 minutes for 5000 metres (13:58.2 in 1942) and a world record holder for the mile (4:01.4 in 1945). Credit: Associated Press Ltd.

You will note that I don't use the words *intervals* or *repetitions* because this overlays fartlek with structure, yet again. OK, it may be semantics, but think about it. How many of you feel comfortable running without a watch or not knowing there is a set pace or distance you have to run, or when you are going to start your next surge? Not many I'd guess.

For me, a typical fartlek session might incorporate 60 minutes running of 15 minutes steady from home, up to 30 minutes of surges at varied pace and distances on parkland, and 15 minutes easy back home. Or if I have the time, I drive to a parkland venue and work it from there. When I warm up for fartlek, I don't really know how many surges I'm going to do or for how long. The only definite is the middle 15 to 30 minutes will be fartlek, and I won't know how I feel until I start the fartlek. In my book that is how it should be. However, a word of caution is warranted. Generally speaking, older athletes require longer warm ups to ensure a safe and adequate adjustment to fast running.[50]

Experts such as Martin & Coe doubt the value of fartlek for the less experienced athlete, instead opting for structure.[51] However, this underestimates the value of fartlek as a progressive system that assists the improvement of the less experienced, or mature, athlete in a gradual fashion. It's a perfect system for an ongoing build in performance year to year. If managed in this way it should enable consistent fast sessions for mature athletes in their 50s and beyond, with less risk of injury.

Mona fartlek[52] is a great concept and would probably suit the elite 'Just Forties' but it's not what I'm looking for as a mature runner guarding against injury. The set structure of this approach is anathema to fartlek devotees, the true believers. You might as well be doing an interval session. Even Moneghetti has dispensed with this 'system' in his later years.[53]

My current Soft Quality Program includes at least one fartlek session per fortnight on parkland terrain, as an additional quality session or sometimes replacing a pre-planned interval session because I can't get to a track or I just feel the need to run fast in natural surroundings after a long day at work. I find it a useful vehicle for race practice, imagining my competitors on my shoulder or coming over the top as I surge past the ghost runners of 'races future'.

To wean yourself onto fartlek I'd suggest you start doing your interval sessions on grass tracks or better still, ovals, without timing your reps or rest breaks. Just because you aren't timing your reps doesn't mean you're not running fast or hard, or can't achieve a quality session. You could even consider running your reps in a park rather than on a track!! I definitely don't want to run fartlek on the roads. If it's on the roads I think it is something else, certainly not fartlek, and watch out for those cars.

There is one thing for certain, the older I get the more fartlek I will do. The change of pace, effort and distance inherent within a session keeps me in touch with the way things were in my youth, if only for fleeting moments and if only known to me.

That is good enough for me, what about you?

A Marriage Made in Hell?

'Training through' isn't talked about much. It's just accepted that is what you need to do. So, I think it's worth getting some things out in the open. Think of your coach or mentor as a marriage counsellor, their advice balancing your need for excitement and instant gratification against the commitment to be in a relationship for the long haul. We navigate our running lives balancing the expectation of just being there for the run, training day in day out, hitting our daily mileage and managing our progression, our maturity, against the ecstasy of a race well performed. But if we don't pay the race the proper attention, respect it, we risk hitting rock bottom.

As we age, we are less inclined to run, let alone compete. The stats tell us so. For those of us who continue to run, some train mindlessly, treating just getting out the door as a major triumph to celebrate in our daily life routine. It's become a chore, drudgery. But it doesn't have to be that way. While our focus is on the long haul, something is missing. To maintain a healthy relationship in our running lives we need to spice things up occasionally with a peak race, or series of races.

I guess what I'm trying to say is let's get fresh, I'm not meaning to be cryptic. Let me tell you a story, and maybe you will understand.

Once there was a runner who was constantly injured, ignoring her counsellor's advice. Due to significant down-time she was always in 'catch up' mode. She developed a perverse mindset of 'training through' races for something into the future and not focussing enough on the present. She took high mileage to the extreme and didn't race enough. When she did race, she raced tired, legs heavy and psychologically drained. She took the race for granted, that it would always be around. Sometimes in a race she felt spasms of absolute ecstasy though never achieved true fulfilment. It wasn't the sensation she desired. She suffered a lack of training continuity at critical times because of her injuries. She was forever frustrated. The relationship with running was turbulent, cooled and finally broke down. There was nothing left in the emotional tank, she was distraught. It was irreconcilable, running ceased altogether and the past relationship became a distant memory of what could have been.

'Training through' is a blight on our sport. Harsh maybe. But when turning up for a race, how many times have you heard someone say things like: 'just having a bit of a hit out today', 'got a bit of a niggle so not going too hard', 'just doing a tempo run, see how I go', 'wearing my heavy trainers, not really racing today', 'did a long run yesterday, too tired to race fair dinkum'? I understand this is partly about taking an opportunity to run fast without the pressure of competing and that it is also an opportunity to have a social outing, but a race is not meant to be a social outing, where you just participate and don't compete. A race is the zenith, where you give it your all - either to win, place as high as you can, run a fast time, or pull out a personal best if you've got it in you.

If you are reckless, insensitive to the needs and respectful demands of your lifelong partner, running, your relationship can deteriorate, to such a degree that you ignore its ultimate attraction, racing, with all its nuance, the release and fulfilment it can deliver. Racing brings new experiences to the relationship, in new locations, or old locations that provide great memories, of how you romanced the race, danced with others, with energy and vitality, starry eyed, your outlook joyous.

When I reflect on my first running relationship I see many examples of racing surprisingly well on my way back from injury, when I was attempting to patch up my relationship with running. In those moments I was fresh, the excitement was there and the thrill of the chase was heightened by the knowledge that the romance still existed. The issue for me and others I'd guess, is that we carry the relationship too far. We become obsessive. We run to extremes, we overtrain, and we kill the relationship with what we mistake for love, without realising what we've done. Until it is too late. It's a marriage made in Hell.

I'm not able to talk authoritatively about Deek's situation, but from all accounts his experience of 1984 mirrors the classic case of overtraining, the kiss of death, an affair gone wrong. After an upwards trajectory in his love of running when he won all the major marathon races going, from 1981 to 1983 inclusive, he admits this loving relationship became all-consuming. Thinking more is better, he overcooked his Los Angeles Olympic marathon finishing fifth and suffered a total breakdown. Misdirected passion bred staleness and a tailspin in race performance.

Luckily for Deek, by a combination of self-reflection and counselling from Pat Clohessy he was able to quickly repair his relationship with running and racing, pull himself from the depths of despair and win the Boston marathon of 1986 in an Australian best of 2:07:51. This is a performance revered within our distance running fraternity as the archetypal example of an enduring relationship, something to point to for over three decades, the bumps in the training road for Deek all but forgotten, and its anniversaries celebrated.

But for the average runner the hurt can cut so deep that many years are lost before we get to a place where we want to renew our vows. So, we rekindle the love gradually with sensitivity, thoughtful to what we had and with some trepidation, we rebuild the old romance with training and running, loving the race with all our hearts. But not with the obsessive zeal of youth that caused us to overtrain. More with the mindful wisdom of age that allows us to enjoy our running for what it is, and visit the race experience time and again, with the respect it deserves and a greater appreciation of the long haul.

A marriage made in Heaven.

Dietary Dilemma

As a runner I have always been ambivalent about diet and alcohol. When I was younger it was generally 'eat and drink what you want within limits and train hard and she'll be right'. However, in the words of one Cerutty disciple 'the athlete can train every day, but if he is not digesting the proper foods, his training will not be giving him its full benefit'.[54] With age no longer on my side I have become more aware of diet as it relates to nutrition, health and injury recovery, rather than athletic performance per se.

When I read the training books from past eras to current there is one constant in the dietary advice: 'a well-balanced diet is all you need.' But in different eras this meant different things. And as far as I can see, we are now living longer and ageing more slowly. So, such general advice doesn't really help an old codger like me who is gaining girth, and attempting to compete hard while getting older in the 21st century.

In the era of the internet I find dietary advice perplexing, mixing the available science and research with selective facts, consumerism and product marketing on a mass scale. Of course, it suits many of us to disregard reality and grab onto the glitzy promo as the purported factual basis for the diet we want to have rather than what is nutritionally good for us. And believe me, as we get older nutrition does become more important in your thinking, macro and micronutrients, blood and heart health floating to the surface.

Another factor is the dietary supplementation industry. This adds a layer of complexity to our decision making about appropriate diet and nutrition. From the crack pot elixirs of the 1800s to the slick modern-day marketing of vitamins and other 'natural' (but artificially produced) products we are awash with advice about what we need to live life to its best. How do we discern fact from fiction? And let's be honest there is always someone you know whom absolutely swears by something or other that will enhance performance. Therefore, it is only natural that many of us in our desperation to live longer, be healthier and/or improve performance will try anything at least once.

I suppose I am a sceptic about the value of vitamin and mineral supplements, and other additives. Having never used any in my life, in a moment of weakness, in my late fifties, I did embark upon a regular low-level intake of glucosamine with chondroitin as part of an injury recovery process (this substance is a commonplace intake amongst the elderly, athletic or otherwise). In hindsight I'm not convinced it had any more effect than a placebo. Really my life mantra is not to take any supplements unless prescribed for a medically diagnosed condition, and I'm not sure why I strayed from this stance. Maybe it was just pure frustration to seize anything that may help me run again?

When it comes to alcohol, the Australian pre-occupation with alcohol as the pre-eminent lubrication for virtually every social setting is beyond my comprehension. While alcohol may be accommodated in different cultures for different reasons, it is poison to athletic performance and under certain conditions it is known to trigger arrhythmias in athletes.[55] I can point to a period in my early twenties when I ran 13 weeks straight of very high mileage and consumed no alcohol whatsoever. My energy system felt as clean as a whistle, finely tuned to perfection. You could naturally assume this was the effect of the mileage but, sad to say, I know it was the result of total alcohol deprivation.

In my second running career from my late forties into my fifties I graduated to a wider variety of fresh fruit and vegetables, less red meat (but still regular), more fish and nuts. And I just love my dairy products, particularly cheese and milk. Consuming dairy is something I will continue into my seventies to supercharge my body's ability to preserve bone strength, prevent osteoporosis and reduce the prospect of injury. I definitely eat less canned and packaged or processed foods. While I still eat my fair share of rubbish foods as add on snacks, I have significantly reduced the proportion of junk food and sugar.

Entering my sixties, avocados, berries, natural yoghurt and leafy greens have become staples, dark chocolate and red wine managed out, their mythical health properties challenged and disproven. Gone is the 'added salt', replaced by ground pepper. But I've drawn the line at chickpeas. I just can't come at them despite their obvious benefits as a plant-based food, though if it's mashed into a hummus dip, I find it OK. Go figure.

I haven't yet experienced the lack of appetite that is so often mentioned for mature people, that can become concerning to nutritionists. I definitely eat less overall than I did when in my thirties. I drink more water and limit my intake of sports drinks. It requires a conscious effort to remain hydrated, as I could easily go without drinking anything at all, a common consequence of ageing so I'm told. And despite my comments about alcohol, I do enjoy an occasional cold beer but I've become a two-pot screamer.

I have read the articles about maximising recovery and training effect by our choices in food combinations and timing of consumption during and after events, but hell, I'm not competing for sheep stations so I'm a bit lazy when it comes to the practical application of the sports science. And like many, my motivation has been dented by recurrent injury. After all, do you really want to wolf down protein rich food immediately after intensive exercise (strength based or intervals), or just before going to bed, to increase your muscle rebuilding capacity? Noting that the mature athlete generally requires approximately double the calorie intake of a younger athlete to achieve the same effect I'm not sure I could do it.[56]

So, after navigating through all of the available literature and advice about diet and nutrition throughout my life, where do I find myself as a mature runner wanting to be healthy and perform well in the 21st century? Well, I'll tell you. While I think I'm getting a more balanced natural diet I remain confused, and that's the truth. But I'm alive and well and, despite my dietary ignorance, I'm performing OK. You can't really ask for anything more.

My only advice to you, dear reader, is take the time to consult with appropriately qualified professionals to make those crucial decisions about nutrition in your later life circumstance. It is an investment in yourself you can't do without.

Running High

Though many years have passed, the Mexico City Olympics of 1968 remain strong in the Australian sporting psyche. Tainted by the disastrous effects on the Olympic aspirations of sea level endurance athletes these Olympics provided a reference point for world athletics in its future relationship with high altitude training and sporting performance. Who can forget the lost opportunity for Australians like Ron Clarke, Derek Clayton and Kerry O'Brien to compete on an equal footing against their altitude acclimatized competitors? The poignant image of Dr Brian Corrigan holding Ron Clarke in a collapsed state after the 10,000 metres final remains etched in the minds of many Australians of that era.

While altitude training is a controversial topic, sports cardiologist Ben Levine puts it in simple terms: at high altitude 'you draw in less oxygen per breath than you would at lower altitudes.' It is well known that even with acclimatization, and despite a greater perceived effort due to reduced oxygen levels, you cannot train or race as hard at high elevations as at sea level. Paradoxically, if continuously training at altitude, you may be tempted to overtrain to make up for any perceived deficit in training outcomes, which can never be made–up anyway. Just to ram home this point, the USA once recognised the deficit in performance at altitude by having a 3% 'altitude allowance' for entrants to national championships for competition distances of 1500 metres or longer achieved above 4000 feet. Though this does not appear to be currently in vogue.

There is little available information about the implications of altitude training for mature runners. While there appears to be a level of consensus that a younger elites' racing performance may benefit from a live high train low (LHTL) program, many experts point to the variation in individual responsiveness to altitude training ('high' is 8000 feet above sea level and 'low' is 4000 feet or below). Some contend that the relationship between altitude training and improved racing and training performance at sea level can be tenuous. Owen Anderson considers that supporters of altitude training tend to focus on the relationships of heart, muscles and aerobic capacity as paramount to running success, disregarding the significance of the nervous system. Given the ravages of the ageing process I'm not sure that provides me with any reassurance of its potential benefits to mature athletes who have lower VO_2 ceilings and can experience a gradual degradation in nervous system functionality.

There is a body of research that suggests that altitude training would not result in a substantial improvement in race performance for non-elite athletes. The premise of this argument is that benefits from altitude training can only be gleaned if the athlete has a large aerobic base (with enhanced cardio vascular system) built from many years logging high mileage – the assumption being that non-athletes and your average club athlete would not have this bedrock of training to draw upon to maximise their physiological adaptation from altitude training.

I've never been to Falls Creek but I've heard a lot about it. Until recently, I had never trained at any significant elevations though I had travelled through high altitude terrains at different times during my life. In recent years, aged 56-60, I had cause to visit Denver Colorado on four separate occasions for up to three weeks at a time – once in late summer (2015) and twice in midwinter over the Christmas period (2015 and 2016) and lastly in the North American spring month of March (2019).

Denver Colorado is known as the mile high city. Its elevation sits nicely within the range of 4000 to 8000 feet that experts claim is the ideal for altitude training. The city of Boulder, made famous by Frank Shorter, and a once upon a time Deek training stronghold, is close by. During my first visit I was running very short distances, recovering from a nagging knee injury and managed to build my training up to 25 minutes continuous running in the aptly named Rocky Mountain Lake Park. I didn't feel any effects from the altitude, probably because I wasn't running fast enough. During my second visit, four months later, I was nursing an achilles injury, and unable to run, though I did a few weight sessions. I did not notice any difficulty breathing in general day to day living.

However, by my third and fourth visits, during Christmas 2016 and March 2019, respectively, I was in full training, running 50-90 minutes each day. While in Denver I experimented with some faster continuous running over longer distances, and during one run I attempted to crank up the speed, reducing from 5 to 4 minutes kilometre pace. Immediately upon doing so I felt light headed and had to ease back. During my subsequent outdoor runs, I continued to run good pace but not high speed, and felt fine. I tried one session including 3 x 3 minutes strides with long recovery intervals on a dirt path and felt I was moving well. While I never felt any excessive tiredness, I was vigilant in monitoring my physical responses to any change in pace. In hindsight I may have been running slower than normal without realising it (I only ever ran to time, not distance).

Being at altitude, and during Christmas, in the midst of the Rockies, naturally it snowed, and heavily. So, on some occasions towards the end of my trip I had no choice but to run on a treadmill in a gym at my accommodation. This was my first ever experience of treadmill running, and I make no apologies for saying I hated it. However, it did bring a greater focus to my effort, resulting in some indoor running at much faster speeds, with no ill effects. Maybe a level of adaptation to altitude had started to occur?

On each occasion, I returned to Australia none the wiser about the benefits of altitude training but no worse for the experience. Any expectations about super charged performance were rudely shaken by some very average performances at my weekly Newcastle Veterans track competition. However, given I was living high and training high (LHTH) in Denver, rather than training low, I guess it wasn't reasonable to expect any discernible improvement in race performances after only three weeks at altitude. Though soon after returning from my last visit I did manage a one-off higher level track performance, a personal best M60 3km of 10:50. So, maybe it did make a difference?

Thinking about this limited exposure, I had cause to ask whether there is a long-term benefit to living at altitude. There are well-known examples of communities at high altitude with some of the longest living populations in the world. There is some conjecture that their natural inhabitants experience cardiovascular benefits that contribute to such longevity. Maybe something to aspire to? Leave the rat race, and converge upon a Shangri-La like sea change post-employment, and eventually, post running!

A retirement built in heaven, where natural health benefits abound.

No Bugles No Lungs

The air rushes hard against my lungs as I emit gutteral winces of pain. Only 50 to go, third hill rep up Burwood Road, and soon I'll reach the entrance to Scout Camp Road. As I hit atop the rise and stagger off to the left into 'Scout Camp' I imagine myself in Peter Snell's shoes, majestic, powerful, striding up the hills of Auckland as the colossus he was, and then I reflect on my own effort to emulate him, subconsciously at least, for I am barely conscious. But I know he is there by my side.

While Snell continues with his recovery jog atop the hill, I let him go. Legs astride, hands on knees, bent over sucking in the big ones I gradually regain awareness of my surroundings. As I look up, I see a recreational walker coming towards me, along the dirt that is Scout Camp Road. With spit hanging from my chin and still reeling from my effort, she looks at me quizzically, as though questioning what this old man is doing. She passes without a word, not even acknowledging my presence.

Slowly, as the anaerobic haze dissipates, the need to complete the fourth and final 300 rep seeps back into my consciousness. I start my recovery jog for the next rep. Like a Thunderbirds marionette I teeter down the hill, one eye ahead, one eye on the road watching for approaching cars. Not sure I'll get through it but hoping I will. Impatient, Snell already strode his way down the hill.

Landing at the bottom I wait for Snell to complete his sprint rep on the flat before doing a quick about turn at the Yuelarbah Trail entrance to Glenrock Reserve, to start my last hill rep. My willingness to hurt myself is there, it still burns strong within. This is reassuring as I charge through the first 50 metres of my final rep for it is so easy to doubt myself and bail, take the easy way out. I nearly always think about it, especially during those first 50 metres. Gaze affixed 10 metres ahead, my arms pumping hard, I run eyes wide shut, impervious to the hurt to come but knowing it will arrive.

OK, this is supposed to be about form and building strength and flexibility, and not about pure speed. That comes later in the program. But it doesn't feel that way as I ease into my final rep. Snell is on my shoulder and he's urging me to go harder, then he's past, gone in no time at all. Snell is prancing, bouncing, his distinctive black and white road trainers propelling his sturdy frame like a juggernaut. Just 12 more reps for him to complete! But for me, by the 200 mark in this my fourth rep, I'm sprinting flat out just to keep up. And as I try to go with Snell it happens: the legs melt into the tarmac, the stride length shortens, the arms start flailing and finally the throat sears as the lungs deprived of sufficient oxygen no longer work. But I get there, one helluva mess with my session completed, my distance running integrity intact, in awe of Snell and others like him. A wry smile, I got through it with Snell's help.

With chest heaving, my thoughts immediately turn to my next planned hill session. A 3km sustained hit out on the Redhead to Whitebridge section of the Fernleigh track, as part of my regular 20km training run. I contemplate the undulations of the Dandenong Mountains, the infamous two-mile hill, and the stomping ground for Ron Clarke and others of the Ferny Creek Gang. I think about Snell's first experience of completing Waiatarua when he broke down and cried. I won't be doing that but I'm much older now, not running quite as far or as hard though I like to think I am. And I'll definitely need the help of the Ferny Creek Gang to get through this next session, no doubt about it.

Running hills is tough but has great rewards. Pardon the pun, but one way or another, hills are steeped in the Australasian running traditions of Cerutty, Lydiard and Clarke. For the mature runner, hill running can be a highly beneficial way of improving speed. While a structured training program often supports a specific phase of intensive hill work, a continued emphasis on hills throughout a yearly program can assist the older runner in maintaining a degree of leg strength and power. Regular continuous runs on hilly courses can also provide durability for race performance that is hard to surpass.

The lower aerobic capacity of mature runners is more discernible when running hills than any other type of training. It will find you out quicker than you may expect. You need to be careful. The focus should be on form and building leg strength, at no harder than medium effort.

One thing is for sure, as I look forward to my own hill training, I won't be blowing any bugles, not with the lungs I own.

Stuck on Four

I'm stuck on four, sub-four is no more. I said to my wife when I can't average better than four minutes kilometre pace for 5km I will revert to casual running for fitness and health and give up competition. With wrinkled nose and raised eyebrows, she just shrugged it off as another promise she knew I wouldn't keep.

I can't fathom it, whether its 3km or 10km, or even a bit longer, my pace is consistent at a smidge over four. I'm like a metronome moving through the ages, my slow twitches overwhelming what's left of my fast twitch muscles, sapping my ability to accelerate, sprint or even maintain a half decent pace. Running in quicksand, I'm sinking ever faster the harder I try.

I was expecting it would be at 65 but it got me earlier, at 63. Oh, what will I do? I can't retire now. Well, I've thought it through and devised a plan. I won't tell her because I'm crafty and I don't want to look a fool if it doesn't work out. And besides, I can't stop running, I just won't. But I'm confident it will be right in the end. What could go wrong?

As you'd expect, I've sought advice, I've done my research. And yes, it is possible, to reverse this trend, at least in the short term, or maybe mitigation is a better description. The experts tell me so. But it won't be easy to claw back the speed, to re-energise myself. I've got enough fast twitches left, just enough, to bring it all back.

So, what exactly do the experts say? Yes, we all know that we lose muscle mass as we age, and significantly so into senior years if we don't do anything about it. Many of us are sick of hearing about it, but what can we do to forestall the inevitable loss of speed? Our fast twitch to slow twitch muscle fibre ratio cannot be changed through training, but our ability to get the best out of our fast twitches can. To run fast we need to train fast by including a regular component of higher intensity running in our program throughout the whole year, ongoing. 'Use it or lose it' is definitely the mantra.

Around age 40, men start to lose testosterone, women lose estrogen, the effect on men's loss of muscle being larger than women's loss. And on top of that, there is a decrease in hormones related to muscle maintenance and development. There will likely be no change in your weight because, even for the most dedicated, the loss of muscle is being masked by an increase in body fat, a change in body composition.[57] It is just a matter of degree. And it gets better. The increase in body fat, and reduction in muscle mass, which is of a poorer quality anyway, reduces your VO2max![58]

Hey so I'm 64, how does that apply to me? Well, this means that if I don't do anything to mitigate the loss of muscle, I will get slower and slower and shrivel into a skeletal mass of non-performing arms and legs, gasping for air, and maybe with an extended gut to boot. Something to look forward to! Do I need to re-examine my diet? Is that the key that unlocks the door to performance enrichment. Well sure, my additional intake of protein will help my muscles out, but will it really make much difference? Only time will tell.

And don't forget about your arms, your biceps. I've heard it said that runners over 65 years of age may suffer a significant loss of motor units (a group of muscles fibres activated by a single nerve) in their arms, actually the same loss as experienced by sedentary older non-runners, if not strengthening their arms.[59] Wow I can hear you say, your exasperation echoing in my ears, as my head spins with these thoughts and my will is steeled for a future war with my body.

It's a war with nature we can never totally win, but we can have small victories along the way as we battle it out, to infinity and beyond. And so, if I get back under four, which I will, it will be an achievement of gigantic proportions to be celebrated as one for the ages. A last attempt to regain some semblance of racing dignity before it all goes to pot.

And when it's gone, when it is all said and done, and I just can't beat it, fast twitch be damned, I'll just run, run steady, run long, into my twilight years, happy that I outfoxed mother nature for a short time, until I could run no more.

Where Have All the Runners Gone?

I look on with astonishment at the dysfunction around me. We are living longer but our quality of life is questionable. We rely on automation, technology and a caring army to get by. But do we really get by?

The stats are thrown at us, 50% of the adult population is sick one way or another: heart, cancer, mental health, dementia. How can that be?

I compare past and current levels of age grade participation and it remains low into the sixties. No matter where in Australia, or where in the world, this is a truism. The amenity of modern civilisation combined with the wonders of medical science are not even making a dent on the activity levels of the Grey Brigade. Sure, there are parkruns, but delve into the results and you will see that no-one much past 60 years of age is participating. Despite the hype that this is not so, it is so. Plain as the nose on your face.

There are women and men of the mature set, even those more senior, running superlative race times but they are few and far between. They get the plaudits but before the Veterans movement started there were men, granted no women, who were running fast into their sixties. Their performances have been lost in the mists of time, as each generation forgets the achievements of those who came before them, old or young.

Why do we give in so easily to the ravages of ageing? Our life is starting at 60 but we cow-tow to the doomsayers. Why?

50 is the new 40 or so I thought. But maybe I'm just disregarding the truth of it all, that it can never be so. Then again, in retirement from work, we have the opportunity to breathe clean air again, free from the push and pull of 24/7 demands on our time, to devote time to living and just being.

I always worked to live not lived to work, something that is anathema to the capitalists, the captains of industry that drive consumerism for consumerisms sake, in a world where materialism is valued more than life itself.

Well, I for one say, just give me a pair of shorts and some running shoes and let me loose on the coastal bush trails. And all will be right in the world, if only for those moments in time when I am lost in my thoughts and contemplations of life. May it ever be so.

Fool for A Coach

My coach is a pain in the arse

He is always there urging me on, in training and racing, at the track, on the roads or country

I can't get away from him, he travels everywhere with me

He is overbearing and thinks he knows it all

He has got a good heart but he doesn't quite know what he's doing

He is not accredited, though he's well-read so he does have some knowledge about exercise physiology

He won't take advice from others

He doesn't have a squad so I'm the centre of his attention

He does the sessions with me and I just can't shake him

He times everything I do and gets upset if I don't hit target pace

He sets unrealistic goals and keeps changing them

He argues with me about training schedules

He makes me train twice a day and I don't like it

He makes me train in extreme heat and cold and I don't like it

It's his way or the highway

He's a boring fart and has no social life

He only talks running

He has no friends, only acquaintances

He never takes time out, only if he's forced to

He makes me run when I'm injured

He won't let me freshen up for races

He thinks he knows my strengths but he doesn't

He thinks he knows my weaknesses but he doesn't
He thinks he is a great race tactician but he isn't

He takes all of the credit if I win
He accepts none of the responsibility if I lose
He thinks he knows what I'm capable of, but he doesn't know me
He is my conscience, but he doesn't really know me
He screams at me in frustration
He doubts me all the time
My coach is a fool
My coach is me

Women

If I were a woman, what would I say about how things are for women's distance running? That's how I was planning to start this piece, with a schmaltzy title like *Ladies Lament* or *In Her Shoes*, both hackneyed phrases, but, er, it's hard to come up with brand new titles, never penned, seen or heard before, that can attract the reader. So, I finally decided on the title you see before you, a simple word with mammoth complexity. It's a conundrum that needs explaining.

I really want to write about women, but it's a minefield for us men. The ease with which we fall into misogynistic, patriarchal writing is alarming. And how can I really write about a woman, what she feels, how she views the world, where she sees the sport and herself in twenty years' time and where she has come from? I've accepted that I can't.

But I still want to write about them, women, that is. Not females, women. For some writers the use of 'female' to describe women is not on, particularly if used as a noun. Use of 'man/men' and 'woman/women' is more appropriate in this day and age. Accusations of sexism swirl around the use of 'female' and 'male', that relate to biological sex, whereas use of the term woman and man relates to gender, a 'whole human person'. So now even when adjectifying (is that a word?) I seek to use 'woman' and 'man' as much as practically possible. It's a sign of respect to both genders that as a writer I make this effort, but I'm particularly sensitive to not offending women, given their long history of discrimination and put downs.

How is it that many of the early writings about women's running, what it means to them, how they train, and their aspirations, were actually written by men, and largely still are? Why is it that many women's team sport coaches are men? Is it because women don't have the knowledge or skill set? I don't think so. Or women aren't assertive enough, they just go with the flow? Do they wince at such a suggestion and just get on with the doing, as practical women do? Letting the man play the game he wants to play, allowing him to think he is in control but holding all the power in her own hands? I'm not really sure we are there yet. These questions pull at me like a young child tugging at my shirt tails.

Allison Roe winning the 1981 Boston Marathon by 8 minutes in 2:26:46. Credit: Betsey Rounseville.

I want to write about the grace of an Allison Roe, the elegance of a Greta Waitz, the tenacity of a Kerryn McCann and the class of a Faith Kipyegon. But I can't. I'm afraid. Afraid I'll say the wrong thing. Afraid I'll disrespect the woman without knowing it. Afraid of my own ignorance. And if I start talking about mature women, well that's in another stratosphere, out of my league, well out of my comfort zone, a writer just waiting to crash and burn. But I do want to talk about the consistency of Jessica Stenson, the perseverance of Joyce Smith, the flow of Joan Benoit-Samuelson, where they came from and how their deeds inspire us, their thoughts, their achievements, and how they got by, then and now.

Do I really want to dive into the mire of the mature woman and all that goes with that? Yes, I want to understand, but do I need to spread the word on these issues? Isn't it already being spread by women to other women? Why do I need to talk about it? Well, actually, maybe men do need to know and appreciate all that women have to cope with, and manage, overcome and absorb to deliver superb lifetime performances while other things are bubbling away under their skin. But we need women to talk to men, about women, and what they want, more and more, not men to talk about women when they don't really have a clue - don't you think so? Men have only scratched the surface of their own primitive urges to have a go, whereas women dig much deeper into their desire to compete, peeling away the layers of social prejudice as they go, managing complex biological changes throughout their lives, and all the time fending off men's endemic patronising behaviour.

The women I relate to, old and young, cuss, fart, spit, sweat, grunt, groan and hurt like all of us, men. They are ferocious in spirit like Atalanta, the Greek Goddess of Running. You know the story of this young woman's single-minded approach to life, who valued her freedom above all else, reflecting an ancient Crete tradition of athletically empowered women exercising free choice in their selection of husbands and lovers. And running like the wind, beating all the men, only succumbing to defeat from a suitor by virtue of an orchestrated process involving golden apples and a father who disliked his daughter because she had not been born a boy.[60]

A good story, yes? But when I examine it objectively, this is an ancient take on the subjugation of women, putting her in a straitjacket and demanding conformity to a man's world. Much like the athletic systems in place that sit around the globe, right now, right below your noses - strong and sturdy programs, held up by yesterday's pillars of manhood, supported by an inherent male bias and not exactly a right fit for the womanhood of today.

Despite continuing poor systems of support and encouragement, where women are continually expected to fit into a man's world, we have independent women. That's right, that's where we are now, racers, myth breaking mothers and daughters, sisters and aunts, and even grandmothers, pounding the streets, putting on their spikes, tearing over the hills, and beating the men of yesteryear.

So, there you have it. Once again, I have talked about women, though it was not my intention and I am not qualified to do so. Because, well, despite my lack of knowledge, I just can't help myself - after all I am a man - as I watch in amazement the women endurance athletes of today edging their way towards the performances of tomorrow that will nearly match the best of the men.

It's an evolutionary process on fast forward for all to see.

The Ghost of Cinders Past

The record breakers of years gone by did it tough. They raced on cinders and grass, often cut up, one lane wide to get some traction. Soft tracks, powdery and sometimes crumbling surfaces, or rock hard, cracked, wet grass, bare dirt, no give or too spongy, mud caked spikes. But there is little acknowledgement of these difficult conditions. The record books don't say world record run in a quagmire, or raced in lane two, or spikes were too long (or short), or slippery conditions. And don't get me started on footwear, technology replacing effort these days!

Many of the past greats, more than the modern runner realises, raced barefoot and taped, because the tracks didn't suit the wearing of shoes. Even in major national and international championship events. It's as though the global keepers of the stats are oblivious to these issues, treating records run past and present on equal footing.

Granted, training could be hit and miss, mental toughness coming to the fore to compensate for any lack thereof. The spirit indomitable and its effect under-appreciated, training systems still evolving. The images of the 1940s, 50s, 60s and pre-World War II years where mud is splattered neck high across the racer's vest, faces peppered with shale and grit, as they thrash through pools of water, are a thing of the past. The all-weather tracks put paid to those rough and tumble battles glorious, a scrap in the muck, a tussle on the grass. You'll never see their like again, unless of course you happen to be a spectator of cross country, or better yet a competitor. The modern-day elites, not a patch on the racers of ye by-gone days, expect manicured grass lands, smooth rolling hills and dry conditions as a given. You hear the mutterings if there is a bit of mud, or rain, or God forbid, a steep hill, fence or creek to overcome.

At this point, I beg the readers pardon, because I've gone a bit off script. Got carried away as I do. I guess what I'm trying to say is they are a soft bunch, these track racers of today. Consider this, Ron Clarke ran two great 10000 metre track races in his career. His world record 27:39.4 of 1965 at Oslo's Bislett stadium was achieved from the front on a cut up cinder track, running 'wide much of the time' in windy conditions. Three years later he raced an extraordinary 27:49.4 on Crystal Palace's tartan track in atrocious conditions, number blown from his singlet and all alone. This was six weeks before the 1968 Olympics, where he was robbed of a fair race at Mexico City.

Ron Clarke on his own in front during his world record 10000 metres in Oslo 1965. Credit: Knut Edvard Holm.

It took three more years before someone else broke 28 minutes, 1971 bringing in a trickle of sub-28s' led by a young Dave Bedford hitting 27:47 at Portsmouth, and a European 10000 metres championship race gone mad in Helsinki, both on synthetic tracks. It was another year before the floodgates opened and Lasse Viren broke Clarke's record, admittedly after a fall, in the battleground of the Munich Olympic final.

Clarke loved tartan the best stating that Crystal Palace's tartan surface gave him at least a 30 second improvement on that blustery night. Ordinarily, in calm conditions Clarke estimated that a synthetic track gave him an advantage of 15 to 20 seconds for a six miles effort. But I think he was cautious in his outlook, partly because of his tendency to understate his own ability and achievements. Hell, Clarkie barely acknowledged the poor track condition at Oslo contributing to a slower time than he could have run, instead applauding the support of the crowd as a positive influence to his world record time. Now that's modesty of the highest order.

Examining his world record performance, you would have to say he lost 1-2 seconds per lap purely due to the condition of the track. Let's split the difference and make it 1.5 seconds. That means that Clarkie ran very close to 27 minutes flat that night (a 2.25% benefit for 27:01.9 if you do the math), in real terms, or by my definition of real terms.

If you read widely there are hints about the difference between cinders and synthetic, hidden in the threads of distance running chat rooms and internet published studies, innocuous and guarded in their conclusions, heatedly debated and reluctantly agreed that there is a difference. But I take my lead from the runners themselves, with a respectful disregard to Clarkie's assessment, because he was just too self-effacing. Bob Schul, Olympic 5000 metres winner in Tokyo 1964 is not backward in his opinion that there is a two second difference per lap in the 5000 metres event. And I think he's right, and at the risk of getting too carried away, for the 10000 metres it may be an even greater difference when you factor in the longer you go the more fatigue plays a part in affecting style and efficiency. I note that others have demurred a difference of one second per lap when you drop down to the mile.

Applying my reasoning, Clarkie's Oslo race was truly a once in a generation performance that would have lasted until 1993 had he raced on a synthetic track that evening. If you accept my conservative assessment that 1.5 seconds per lap is a realistic 'difference', no-one ran comparatively faster than Clarke until Yobes Ondieki became the first to break 27 minutes that year. And Clarkie's world record is still comparatively better than Jack Rayner's Australian record of 27:09.57, despite all the hype.

Now that's something, isn't it? Something to be truly appreciated but for reasons that I can't put my finger on, isn't quite understood in this way. 'Too many variables' is the inevitable response from the current crop, 'depends on the runner, depends on their style, their physique, their height, the runner's natural bounce and the track surface' to mask the truth of it all, hiding themselves from the fact that their modern racing credentials don't quite stack up to the heroes of yesteryear. They are not frauds, just ignorant of the class that went before them. Who can blame them for living in the now?

After thinking this through, I got to doodling, drawing some comparisons about existing world records and how the current elites would fare if forced to run on the tracks of the past. Theoretical you may say, rubbery I know, but it's worth a look. Joshua Cheptegei's world record of 26:11 bears some examination. Let's not complicate it too much. I know Cheptegei's base pace is faster than Clarke's but if you apply a 1.5 second 'penalty' (a negative conversion factor) per lap to his world record you will find that if he had raced Clarkie at Oslo in 1965, he would have run about 26:48.5 on cinders, not too much faster than Clarkie would have run on a synthetic track back then.

Given the conditions under which both races were run (Cheptegei's ideal, Clarke's suboptimal) I think this is an accurate reflection of the relative merits of each race performance. And when you factor in the more favourable weather conditions and pacing support for Cheptegei's race, arguably his world record is only marginally faster than Clarke's 1965 world record, in my comparative terms, not the 88.4 seconds faster indicated by the record books.

Comparing apples with oranges, I know, but it gives you a sense of how far the modern-day athlete has not progressed in nearly 60 years of racing and technology evolution. Or maybe it gives a sense of how far ahead Clarkie really was, gob smacking stuff.

So, I'm sorry to burst your bubble but applying this negative conversion factor we see that the modern day elite ain't all they are cracked up to be - at least the men. The women have only competed on synthetic tracks for distance running since 1969, with no legitimately recognised history in the racing of events greater than 800 metres beforehand.

By my observation the crunch and grunt of cinders has been replaced by the soulless pitter patter of synthetic surfaces, delivering faster times but not intrinsically better performances. And as my rubbery legs, and powerless excuse for ankles, propel me around my local grass track (they still exist) I contemplate the magnificence of racers like Ron Clarke, what they had to deal with, and how they inspired a generation, despite running on 'goat tracks'.

And hey, that's got me thinking, how do grass track surfaces really compare to cinders to synthetic? And what about the modern day four-minute synthetic milers? In my estimation they are only 4:04ers, great pretenders that haven't actually broken four minutes based on the blood and guts, heart and soul rampaging performances of the milers of the 1950s and 60s.

Let's rewrite the record books I say, and the rankings..... in reverse. And see where that takes us.

Or maybe that's a headache for another day?

References, Sources and End Notes

Soft Quality Dissected: A Masters Dimension

1 Interview with Peter Reaburn, *Maximising Health & Performance of the Masters Athlete*, Episode 215,

The Physical Performance Show, posted by Runners Tribe 1 June 2020 - https://www.runnerstribe.com/podcasts/maximising-health-performance-of-the-masters-athlete/

2 Reaburn, P, *The Masters Athlete*, Info Publishing Pty Ltd Qld, 2009, p182

3 Reaburn, 2009, p181

The Just Forties

4 Henderson J, (ed) Running After Forty, 1971, article titled *Keep the Kids Out* (David Pain), Runners World Booklet of the Month No. 5, p16

5 Bannister R, *Twin Tracks*, The Robson Press London, 2014, p65

Built to Last

6 *No 'freak', says female Olympian*, The Morning News, Wilmington Delaware, Feb 8 1974, p30, also cited in The Female Runner, Runners World Monthly Booklet No. 34, 1974

7 Fee, E, *The Complete Guide to Running How to Become a Champion from 9 to 90*, Meyer and Meyer Sport (UK) Ltd, 2005, p35

Ullyot, J, *Women's Running*, World Publications, 1976, pp88-89

The Female Runner, p18-19

8 Van Aaken, E, *Van Aaken Method*, Runner's World Magazine, 1976, p89

9 Utzschneider, C, *Mastering Running*, Human Kinetics, 2014, p26

10 Reaburn, 2009, p72

11 Heinrich, B, *Why We Run, a Natural History*, Harper Collins reprint, 2002, p117-118

12 Van Aaken, 1976, p89

13 Utzschneider, 2014, p21

14 http://runnersconnect.net/running-training-articles/how-much-does-age-effect-running-performance

In Search of the Real Sensation

15 Links through Wikipedia search: *Out of Body Experience*, Internet 14 February 2016

16 *Tale of the Ancient Marathoner: Jack Foster's Own Story*, Runners Monthly Booklet No 41, November 1974, World Publications CA

Nowhere to Hide

17 Anderson, O, *Running Science*, Human Kinetics, 2013, p546

18 Burfoot, A, *The Principles of Running: Practical Lessons from my First 100,000 Miles*, Runner's World, 1999, p126

Join the Club? That's Not Entertainment aka An Open Letter to Nobody

19 Jackson C, *Colin Jackson, The Autobiography*, BBC Books, 2004, p23-24

Personal Bests: The Grey of It All

20 Horwill, F. (2003) *Knowing at what age an athlete is likely to achieve peak performance is a big help in planning a training programme* [WWW] http://www.brianmac.co.uk/articles/scni3a2.htm [Accessed 17/12/2015]

21 Lenton, B, Ron Clarke, interview conduct 15 May 1979 at Cheltenham Victoria, Australia, published in Fun Runner, July 1979, Vol 1, No6

Weights for Weights' Sake

22 Anderson, 2013, p253

23 Gaudette J, *Should Distance Runners Lift Heavy?* http://running.competitor.com/2014/02/training/should-distance-runners-lift-heavy_67606

24 Beck K, *Run Strong*, Human Kinetics, 2004, p110

25 Beck, 2004, p110

26 Davis J, *The Benefits of Strength Training for Distance Runners*, http://runnersconnect.net/running-training-articles/benefits-of-strength-training-for-runners/

27 Fee, 2005, p371

28 Utzschneider, 2014, p115

29 Goater J & Melvin D, *The Art of Running Faster*, Human Kinetics, 2012, p142

Feet: A Cautionary Tale

30 Vonhof, J, *Fixing Your Feet, Injury Prevention and Treatment for Athletes*, Wilderness Press, 2016, 6th edition, pp25-26

31 Heinrich, 2002, p160

32 Doheny, Kathleen, *Should Older Runners Embrace the Barefoot Craze?* Health Day News for Healthier Living, 24 March 2015

33 Fee, 2005, p269

34 Subotnick, S, *The Running Foot Doctor*, World Publications, 1977, p36

A Man for All Ages

35 Lenton, B, *Off the Record*, 1981, p64

36 Lydiard A & Gilmour G, *Run to The Top*, Herbert Jenkins Ltd London, 1962, p47

37 Lenton, 1981, p64

38 Pennington J, *The Lydiard Way*, Australasian Track & Field Athletics, Apr 1979, p18

39 Lydiard A. & Gilmour G, *Run the Lydiard Way*, Hodder and Stoughton, 1978, pp54-83

40 Lydiard & Gilmour, 1978, p43

41 Lydiard & Gilmour, 1978, p62

42 Lydiard & Gilmour, 1978, p71

43 Lydiard & Gilmour, 1978, p67

44 Lydiard & Gilmour, 1978, pp80-81

45 Lydiard & Gilmour, 1978, p57

A Matter of Balance

46 Vonhof, 2016, p263

47 Carter, K, online running blog within The Guardian Lifestyle Section, 6 March 2015, https://www.theguardian.com/lifeandstyle/the-running-blog/2015/mar/06/joyce-smith-i-stopped-running-at-74

48 Vonhof, 2016, p263

The Ultimate Free Form

49 Goater & Melvin, 2012, p25

50 Friel, J, *Fast After 50*, Velopress, 2015, p117

51 Martin, D. E. & Coe, P, *Better Training for Distance Runners*, 2nd Edition, Human Kinetics, 1997, p228

52 As reported in many publications, a Mona fartlek session would typically consist of: 2×90sec, 4×60sec, 4×30sec, 4×15sec with a slower tempo recovery of the same time between each repetition; taking 20 minutes in total.

53 Based on electronic communication between the author and Steve Moneghetti on 17 October 2022

Dietary Dilemma

54 Myers, L, *Training with Cerutty*, World Publications, 1977, p49

55 Fee, 2005, p305

56 Friel, 2015, pp221-223

Running High

Corrigan B, *The Life of Brian: Confessions of an Olympic Doctor*, Australian Broadcasting Corporation, 2004, pp80-94

Levine B, *How high-altitude training can benefit elite endurance athletes like runners and swimmers*, 21 November 2016 https://utswmed.org/medblog/high-altitude-training

Anderson, 2013, pp205-211

Hawley J & Burke L, *Peak Performance*, Allen & Unwin, 1998, pp167-175

Martin & Coe, 1997, pp240-246

No Bugles No Lungs

Clarke R & Trengove A, *The Unforgiving Minute*, Pelham Books, 1966

Lydiard & Gilmour, 1962

Lydiard & Gilmour, 1978

Snell P & Gilmour G, *No Bugles No Drums*, Hodder and Stoughton,1965

Stuck on Four

57 Friel, 2015, p92

58 Noakes, T, *Lore of Running*, fourth edition, Human Kinetics, 2002, p84

59 Friel, 2015, p93

Women

60 de Traci, R, *Facts and Myths about Atalanta*, Goddess of Running, published by ThoughtCo. 16 July 2019,

https://www.thoughtco.com/greek-mythology-alanta-1525976

The Ghost of Cinders Past

Clarke & Trengove, 1966, pp147 149

Schul, R, & Krause, R, *In the Long Run*, Landfall Press, 2000, p193

Hendershott, J, editor, *Ron Clarke Talks Track*, tafnews, 1972, pp46-47

What a joy to read. Factually and scientifically-based, Mike has also blended science with the art of ageing as an athlete to this great read.

The book took me back to the fun run era of the 1970's and 80's. Then, like Mike, I was a young athlete who thought older runners were wasting their time competing against the speed, power and endurance of youth. As I matured physically and the mind opened to wisdom gained through experience, I realised that older athletes are smart athletes. They have learnt to listen to their bodies, to train more effectively, to recover harder, to eat smarter, and stay injury-free without hurting themselves. They have learnt what works for them. They are driven by what motivates them. They have become wisened!

In this collection of readings, Mike has eloquently and intelligently shared his wisdom gained through a lifetime of competitive running and deep thinking on what it's like to run as a mature athlete. I loved the read and know you will too.

Peter Reaburn PhD

Retired Professor of Exercise and Sport Science

My love of sport and athletics began prior to the 1956 Melbourne Olympic Games. I was especially motivated and inspired by John Landy and the global chase to achieve the first sub 4 minute mile. John's rivalry with Roger Bannister and others, followed by those Games, made a dramatic impression on me and many youngsters 'back in the day'.

In those days resources for aspiring athletes were not easy to find. My 'gospel' when I first began running was *Franz Stampfl on Running* and I followed Franz's training schedules meticulously. While I was fortunate to have a number of senior club members as mentors, most of my early athletic career was a result of hit and miss training and running strategies. These days athletes are much better off – with a great many books on athletics, instant access to resources, and capable and experienced coaches.

The contribution of Mike and his family to our sport has been invaluable. His father Jim was an excellent running coach and the work of Mike in compiling this book provides a wonderful addition to the resources now available to aspiring and developing athletes of mature vintage and younger.

The range of topics covered should answer a great many questions and see our sport continue to develop. This book will be a most valuable and relevant addition to the material presently available.

Trevor Vincent

OAM, OLY

Born in Liverpool England in 1934, Jim Beisty was a lifetime distance runner and a well performed club athlete. After immigrating to Canada with his family in 1963, the Beistys moved to Melbourne, Australia in 1968. Four years later they settled in Newcastle, New South Wales, where Jim was a founding member of one of the first Veterans (now known as Masters) athletics clubs in regional Australia. He ran 27 marathons throughout his life, 17 under three hours and his best of 2:33:09 at St Hyacinthe in Canada in 1964. His last sub-3 was a 2:59:33, aged 51. Self-educated in exercise physiology, and a Lydiard disciple, Jim coached and influenced many state and national class distance runners in Newcastle and its surrounds from the late 1970s into the 2000s. His coaching was done for love, not for money.

THE END